THE CHILDREN OF CAPTAIN GRANT

Borgo Press Books Translated by FRANK J. MORLOCK

Anna Karenina: A Play in Five Acts, by Edmond Guiraud, from the Novel by Leo Tolstoy

Anthony: A Play in Five Acts, by Alexandre Dumas, Père

The Children of Captain Grant: A Play in Five Acts, by Jules Verne and Adolphe d'Ennery

Crime and Punishment: A Play in Three Acts, by Frank J. Morlock, from the Novel by Fyodor Dostoyevsky

Falstaff: A Play in Four Acts, by William Shakespeare, John Dennis, William Kendrick, and Frank J. Morlock

Jesus of Nazareth: A Play in Three Acts, by Paul Demasy

Joan of Arc: A Play in Five Acts, by Charles Desnoyer

The Lily in the Valley: A Play in Five Acts, by Théodore Barrière and Arthur de Beauplan, from the Novel by Honoré de Balzac

Michael Strogoff: A Play in Five Acts, by Adolphe d'Ennery and Jules Verne

The Mysteries of Paris: A Play in Five Acts, by Prosper Dinaux and Eugène Sue

Peau de Chagrin: A Play in Five Acts, by Louis Judicis, from the Novel by Honoré de Balzac

A Raw Youth: A Play in Five Acts, by Frank J. Morlock, from the Novel by Fyodor Dostoyevsky

Richard Darlington: A Play in Three Acts, by Alexandre Dumas, Père

The San Felice: A Play in Five Acts, by Maurice Drack, from the Novel by Alexander Dumas, Père

Shylock, the Merchant of Venice: A Play in Three Acts, by Alfred de Vigny

The Voyage Through the Impossible: A Play in Three Acts, by Adolphe d'Ennery and Jules Verne

William Shakespeare: A Play in Six Acts, by Ferdinand Dugué

THE CHILDREN OF CAPTAIN GRANT

A PLAY IN FIVE ACTS

by

JULES VERNE & ADOLPHE D'ENNERY

Translated and Adapted by Frank J. Morlock

THE BORGO PRESS

An Imprint of Wildside Press LLC

MMIX

www.wildsidepress.com

FIRST WILDSIDE EDITION

CONTENTS

DEDICATION

To

JEAN-MICHEL MARGOT

For enthusing me for Verne's plays, and assisting me in obtaining this and other rare Verne texts.

CAST OF CHARACTERS

PAGANEL
BURKE
HARRY GRANT
LORD GLENARVAN
AYRTON
BOB
THALCAVE
MULRAY
WILSON
FORSTER
DICK
THE GUIDE
AN OFFICER
AN INNKEEPER
FIRST SAILOR
SECOND SAILOR
A SERVANT
A WAITER
MISS ARABELLA
JAMES GRANT
MARY GRANT
ROBERT GRANT
ELMIRA

SAILORS, NAVAL OFFICERS, CONVICTS, etc.

PROLOGUE

Scene 1

THE SHIPWRECK

The stage represents the tip of a small island; some bushes, some leafless trees, tall rocks to the right and left. The sea beats the point of the isle at the left. At a distance which must be a half mile at sea the remains of a shipwreck can be seen—only the overturned hull is visible. Close to the audience a few barrels and tools saved from the wreck. In the back, the horizon. Broad daylight and the heaven is clear.

All the characters are dressed in bad condition. Some are stretched on the ground, others come and go quickly on the beach. *At Rise*, Captain Grant is standing on a high rock observing the horizon. Ayrton, Forster, and Dick form a group apart. young James is anxiously observing what is going on around him.

FIRST SAILOR (in a deep voice): No, no! Enough of suffering like this.

SECOND SAILOR: To drive so far south is to tempt God.

DICK: It's tempting the devil and the devil doesn't like being tempted! Thus, you see what has become of the *Britannia*!

(Dick points to the hull run aground in the sea and returns to Ayrton.)

FIRST SAILOR: Yes, a hulk which is no longer good for anything and that the first breeze will demolish.

SECOND SAILOR (pointing to Grant with his fist): And all that through the fault of this captain of ill luck!

FORSTER (to Ayrton): You see, Ayrton! Now they are rebelling against Grant. Let's profit by it.

DICK: Yes—and command in his place.

AYRTON: Patience, Forster, patience, Dick. The moment has not yet come, but it is near, and I will pay this man for all I've suffered in my vanity and my interests! Ah, Captain Grant! It's you they entrusted with this mission of going to discover the South Pole in preference to me! It's you they named Commandant of the *Britannia* where I only occupy second place! Well—the shipwreck will do what my will couldn't do. Bad luck to you!

JAMES (aside): What are they up to talking so low? I tremble for my father. It seems to me we are surrounded by nothing but enemies.

FORSTER (to Ayrton): But, why wait any longer?

AYRTON: Because I intend to know, before acting, whose side Harry Grant will take.

FORSTER: And, what side do you want him to take, if not that of leaving this island by whatever means possible, and reaching the lands of the North?

DICK: A barrel of biscuit and a quartet of brandy for twenty-three people. In a week we'll be dead of starvation!

AYRTON: In a few minutes we will know what's going to keep us!

FORSTER: And if the Captain is obstinate in the accomplishment of his plan, which has now become a death threat for the whole crew?

AYRTON: Then it's his own sentence of condemnation he'll be pronouncing.

DICK: And who will take on himself the execution of the sentence?

AYRTON: Who? (pointing to Burke) That brute there who is still roaring in heat and fury.

DICK: Burke?

AYRTON: Yes, Burke, who the Captain had whipped for insubordination! That tiger will avenge himself sooner or later and we will avoid being accused of killing the Captain.

FORSTER: You think he would have the courage?

AYRTON: Him! Wait. (going to Burke) Burke!

BURKE: Huh?

AYRTON: What would you do if the fate of Grant were placed in your hands?

BURKE: I would kill him. (rising and pointing to his fist)

AYRTON (aside) Fine! (in a low voice to the sailors) Ours is a terrible situation, my friends!

FORSTER (low) And it's the Captain who plunged us into it! Bad luck to him!

(Grant has left his post on the height of the rock at the right and placed himself in the midst of the mutineers looking them in the face.)

GRANT: What's this mean?

JAMES (running to him): Oh! Father! Take care!

GRANT: Are you forgetting that I command on this island just as I commanded on the *Britannia*? Here, as on board, I intend to be obeyed by all.

AYRTON: I don't know that any one of us is refusing to do his duty!

GRANT: (severely) None of you, neither officer, nor sailor! I am counting on it! Heaven has harshly tested us, no question, by casting us on this island in the Australian Sea, but nothing is yet desperate. I demand of you only two things: courage which never weakens and unity that nothing can alter. At that price, I will answer for the common well-being and completing our task.

AYRTON: Are you forgetting that the *Britannia* is half broken on the reefs and that it is impossible to refloat it?

GRANT: No, but I know that with zeal and labor we can work to a good conclusion. Dispose everything for a provisional camp. See if we can still save some provisions. Ayrton, embark with some men. You understand me?

AYRTON: (after hesitating) Yes, captain.

GRANT: And you, Forster, watch so that no one touches this case of brandy, perhaps our only reserve.

FORSTER: (looking at Ayrton) Yes, yes! We'll watch!

GRANT: Meanwhile, I am going to inspect this island which I've come to believe is Balker Island in the Australian Sea, situated not far from the coast of Adelaide. Yet once more, my friends, remember, United we are strong. Disunited, we are lost!

JAMES: Father, I'll accompany you.

GRANT: Come, my son. From the height of these rocks we'll take a survey of this island.

AYRTON: And if it is habitable, Captain?

GRANT: If it is habitable, if physical life can be assured, even during the rigorous polar winter we will install ourselves here. From the wreckage of the *Britannia*, in less than six months we will have constructed a ship somewhat smaller, but solid, and once the ice flow reopens, at the first cracking, we will leave this island to search more profoundly, once again, for the route to the south pole.

AYRTON: And if this island is uninhabitable?

GRANT: I will consider. Come, James. (they leave)

FIRST SAILOR: Wait here six months!

SECOND SAILOR: To winter amidst the ice bergs.

FORSTER: To die of hunger.

SECOND SAILOR: And of cold.

DICK: Never, comrades.

ALL: Never!

AYRTON: Eh! Didn't you hear what Harry Grant told you? Your Captain, today as yesterday, here as there. Will you obey?

ALL: No, no.

DICK: When a Captain is crazy, he is removed from his command.

BURKE: Or he's killed without pity or mercy.

FORSTER: He's right! Our captain—it will be you, Ayrton! Long live Captain Ayrton.

ALL: Yes, yes, long live Ayrton.

AYRTON: Comrades, take care of what you are doing! Will you follow me?

FORSTER: Wherever you choose to lead us.

AYRTON: You will obey me?

DICK: Unto death!

AYRTON: Friends, we need a ship, not to go lose ourselves in the polar ice, but to return to the lands of the Pacific. We have the sloop from the *Britannia*. It's a solid craft, well decked, well rigged; and suitable to bring us to the nearest land.

FORSTER: To New Zealand!

AYRTON: No, to Australia. That's where lads with courage, ready for anything can find an independent life, well-being, without pain, riches without labor! There, if we seized a ship for ourselves, it would be a simple thing—on the condition of obeying me.

ALL: In Australia!

DICK: But if the sloop cannot contain more than twenty men—and we are twenty-three.

AYRTON: The sloop will carry only those it can carry.

ALL: How's that?

AYRTON: Harry Grant and his son will stay here. Cold and famine will soon have killed them.

ALL: Yes, yes.

DICK: Let's embark then, and he won't find us on his return!

AYRTON: First of all, load the provisions which have been saved. Perhaps that's all that the *Britannia* can furnish. They will suffice us for a crossing that cannot exceed three weeks. And now, Captain Grant, to the two of us!

(The sailors begin to execute the orders of Ayrton. The barrel of biscuit is rolled towards the sloop which has been brought to the point of the island. The case of brandy is still on stage.)

FIRST SAILOR: Hey! Captain Ayrton, it's getting devilishly thirsty here.

ALL: Oh! Yes, Captain.

AYRTON: Harry Grant forbade you to drink. Well, drink, comrades, drink.

ALL: A drink, a drink.

BURKE: For me, some brandy for me! Since I cannot avenge myself right away, I have to make my rage sleep.

AYRTON: And it will awaken only more terrible, right, Burke?

BURKE: He shed my blood! I will shed his unto the last drop. (drinks)

FORSTER: To the health of the new Captain!

ALL: To the health of Captain Ayrton.

BURKE: To the eternal damnation of Grant (bottle in hand, still drinking) and to his death. (drinks and shivers) To his—

(At this moment Grant appears, he strides towards Burke, snatches the bottle from him and hurls it to the ground.)

BURKE: (rushing on Grant) Sonofabitch!

GRANT: Wretched brute. (repulsing Burke violently; Burke, already drunk, falls) (to Ayrton) Doubtless, Ayrton, it was despite your orders that these wretches are going to lose their reason in intoxication?

AYRTON: It's I who permitted them to drink.

GRANT: You dared?

AYRTON: Go ahead, comrades!

FIRST SAILOR: Drink!

OTHER SAILORS: Drink! Drink!

GRANT: (seizing a hatched) The first of you who touches this case, I split his head open.

FORSTER: (to Ayrton) Well! The moment hasn't come?

AYRTON: Let him go! He's ruining himself.

GRANT: (to the crew) I demanded obedience and union from you in the common interest. This absolute submission to my orders that I impose on my crew, I also impose on my officers. (turning toward Ayrton) Ayrton, you have been given the first example of disobedience! I break you of your rank! You are no longer the mate of the *Britannia*.

AYRTON: What's it matter! There no longer is a *Britannia*.

GRANT: The sloop remains. It's a part of it, and now it's our only means of safety.

FORSTER: (aside) What's he mean?

GRANT: I've just explored this island. It is arid, without vegetation and cannot furnish the physical requirements of a winter harbor. We must leave it, return to the lands of the Pacific, and, since the wind is favorable, we are going to embark this very day.

AYRTON: The sloop can contain only twenty men at most, and there are twenty-three to ship.

GRANT: Three men of the crew will remain on this isle.

SAILORS: Three?

GRANT: I will return myself to get them. In three weeks the sloop will have reached the coast of New Zealand. There I will charter a boat. The ice won't reappear for five months! Then, having five weeks, I will return and we'll see England again; you, your families, me, my dear children that I left there, Mary and Robert.

AYRTON: (interrupting him) And which of us will remain on the island?

ALL: Yes, yes! Which ones?

GRANT: Those that fate chooses. The names will be put in a hat and the first three picked.

AYRTON: (interrupting him) That's unnecessary.

GRANT: What do you mean?

AYRTON: We have already chosen.

FORSTER: Grant and his son, first of all.

ALL: Yes, yes! Grant and his son!

GRANT: Wretches!

AYRTON: (forcefully) The moment has come to choose between Grant and Ayrton.

THE SAILORS: Ayrton! Ayrton!

GRANT: To me, those who are for their Captain.

AYRTON: To me, those who are for Ayrton.

(All the sailors group around Ayrton; Grant is alone with his son.)

ALL: Ayrton!

GRANT: (rushing on Ayrton, axe in hand) Traitor!

JAMES: Father! Father!

(The Sailors rush Grant and disarm him.)

AYRTON: You and your son will stay here on this island—and I am not promising to come get you!

ALL: No! No!

GRANT: I told you no human creature will be found alive here during the winter. Still, for myself, I accept the death you inflict on me. But take my child and leave me alone!

JAMES: (rushing to the arms of Captain Grant) Father, I won't leave you.

AYRTON: Your son will remain with you! And for all the humiliations that I've suffered on your deck, you will drag out, miserably, the few months that remain for you to live! Come on, embark, the rest of you!

GRANT: Ayrton, I won't try to soften you up for me, but for my son, at least have compassion for my son!

JAMES: (hanging on his father) Separate myself from you, father—never! Never! (to Ayrton) Ayrton, I entreat you, I beg you on my knees, don't be without pity, don't abandon us on this desert isle! Think that in Scotland we have my brother and my sister who are waiting for us—two poor orphans who will die of despair when they learn of our deaths! You don't want to soil yourself with so many crimes at once! Mercy, mercy for all of us, Ayrton! Mercy! Mercy!

AYRTON: (a little shaken) No, I—the sentence has been pronounced. Embark, lads, embark.

(The sailors take their place in the sloop and are followed by Forster.

JAMES: (in despair) Lost! We are lost!

GRANT: Wretches! I will find you again, Ayrton! A ship might pass.

AYRTON: (shrugging his shoulders) At the limit of the polar circle? Come off it!

GRANT: I will know how to construct a sloop from the remains of the *Britannia*.

AYRTON: (mocking) With the remains of the *Britannia*? I don't think so, Harry Grant.

GRANT: Ah! (heads towards the sloop)

FORSTER: (to Ayrton) And Burke?

AYRTON: Burke? Since one of us cannot find a place in the sloop, let it be him! (low) In case that cold and famine should spare Harry Grant, that one won't! Make room!

ALL: Keep off!

(The sloop is pushed away and disappears.)

JAMES: (falling on his knees by his father) They are leaving. They are leaving! It's all over. It's all over! Ah, my God! Have pity! Help us.

GRANT: (raising his head) Let's help ourselves, so that heaven will aid us. James, we must leave this island before the ice shuts around it. The wreckage of the *Britannia* is in good condition. But there are only two of us and we need so much time.

JAMES: But, father, during the summer season whalers sometimes approach these shores. Couldn't we?

GRANT: Wait! (stumbling over a bottle that had fallen to the ground) That bottle! A document could be enclosed into it and it could then be thrown into the sea!

JAMES: Perhaps it might be picked up by some ship?

GRANT: And perhaps they will come to save us before time runs out, so long, as will be required for the construction of a new sloop.

JAMES: Yes, father, write! As for me, meanwhile, I am going to prepare a bit of tarpaulin to cork the bottle.

GRANT: (tearing a page from his notebook and writing) "Captain Grant and his son, abandoned on the island Balker, near the Australian lands, after shipwreck of the *Britannia* at latitude 37 degrees south, and longitude 165 degrees west. A long agony awaits them. Come to their aid or they will be lost!"

(Grant takes this paper, folds it and inserts it into the bottle.)

JAMES: (giving him the tarpaulin stopper) Here, father.

GRANT: (closing the bottle) We must, without further delay, go to the beach where the *Britannia* is. Perhaps we'll find some provisions; some clothes. Wood and iron that we can snatch from it will still be our most precious resource!

JAMES: (noticing Burke) Ah! Burke! Abandoned too. Father, he is concerned as we are, in this attempt at salvation.

GRANT: What can you hope for from such a man?

JAMES: Still, allow me—

(At an approving sign from Grant, James approaches Burke, kneels by him, and shakes him gently.)

JAMES: Burke! Burke!

BURKE: What do you want with me? (seeing James) Huh! You, the son of the accursed Captain! Get back. I tell you, get back or if not—

JAMES: Burke, they've all gone, and you, my father and I, have been abandoned!

BURKE: Abandoned! (rising and looking around) Abandoned! Abandoned in this desert!

JAMES: Will you not help us to get out of here?

BURKE: Help you to get out of here, you and your father! (finding himself face to face with Captain Grant) He who had me beaten? Shamefully flogged? No, nothing in common between us—nothing! Nothing except hate and death! (picks up the hatchet while Grant grasps a rifle) Watch out for yourself. I'm on my guard!

JAMES: Father!

BURKE: (leaving) We will see each other again, Harry Grant.

GRANT: Come on, James, to the ship.

JAMES: To the ship, father. (they head toward the back; at that moment there's an explosion and the wreckage of the ship vanishes in the waves) The wretches! They've destroyed what remained of our *Britannia*.

GRANT: (climbing on a rock, bottle in hand) My God! Our only hope is on this fragile bottle, confided to winds and waves!

JAMES: (kneeling) Let it fall, Lord, into helping hands.

(Grant hurls the bottle into the sea.)

CURTAIN

ACT I

Scene 2

CASTLE MALCOLM

The park of Castle Malcolm in Scotland. To the left a pavilion in Anglo-Saxon architecture. A round table with chairs in the garden near the pavilion. A bench to the right.

At Rise, Arabella, Wilson, and Glenarvan are seated around the table on which is a bottle surrounded by petrified materials. Mulray is standing near the table.

ARABELLA: Since this morning I am a bit more calm, a bit less nervous, than usual, tell us, gentlemen, the story of this mysterious bottle.

GLENARVAN: Indeed, this story is very strange and I am going to tell you, auntie.

ARABELLA: Yes, do so, my dear Glenarvan, with all the care possible. You know my temperament is so frail, so sensitive and so delicate.

GLENARVAN: Don't worry, dear aunt, you must know then that this bottle, completely deformed with saline incrustations was found by a crewman of my yacht, the *Duncan*.

WILSON: By Mulray, here present.

MULRAY: Yes, your honor, by me.

ARABELLA: Found. Where was it?

GLENARVAN: In the stomach of a shark, dear aunt.

ARABELLA: Shark! (with terror) Edward! I beg you never to utter the name of that horrible animal before me! They told me the story of an unfortunate man whose head these ferocious fish had eaten.

MULRAY: Head and hat—the story is true, milady.

ARABELLA: And ever since I heard that tale I shudder at only the name of....

MULRAY: Of shark!

ARABELLA: (uttering a scream) Ah!

GLENARVAN: (severely) Mulray!

MULRAY: Pardon! It escaped me, your lordship.

ARABELLA: And you say that this bottle contained an account concerning shipwrecks?

GLENARVAN: Yes, dear auntie, of shipwrecks who are, evidently, lost on some isle in the South Seas. If the bottle had been delivered only to the winds and currents it would never have reached the shores of La Manche! But this shar—

ARABELLA: Stop!

GLENARVAN: But this terrible animal, having swallowed the bottle in distant seas, and having been caught and brought aboard the *Duncan*, we have in this way had news of the unfortunate castaways.

ARABELLA: But how to imagine that the bottle can be found in the stomach of a fish?

GLENARVAN: Sailors are not generally animated by benevolent intentions with regard to the formidable sharks in question. When they catch one, it's customary aboard ship to carefully inspect its stomach. It's done with a few blows of the axe—and it's thus that they found this bottle solidly embedded in the viscera of the one we had caught.

ARABELLA: What a terrifying story. Pass me my flask, my handkerchief, and my fan, Captain Wilson.

WILSON: Here they are, milady.

ARABELLA: (breathing the salts) Continue, my nephew.

GLENARVAN: I was saying that the bottle was examined after it was removed. The incrustations that covered it, these mineral substances under the action of the water proved that it had had a long sojourn in the ocean! Isn't that true, Mulray?

MULRAY: Around ten or twelve months. Your Lordship, having gone to be swallowed in the belly of the shar—

ARABELLA: (terrified) Mulray.

MULRAY: In the belly of—the herring, if Miss prefers this name to the other.

ARABELLA: That doesn't, perhaps, exactly render the thought, but it's less terrifying. I prefer it.

GLENARVAN: In short, it was necessary to use a knife to break the stony envelope of the bottle, in the interior of which we found a paper, unfortunately half eaten up by humidity, and which bore no more than a few—almost indecipherable words.

ARABELLA: But, still—this document?

WILSON: By examining it with care, we came to decipher the name *Britannia*. Lord Glenarvan then researched in the collection of the *Maritime Gazette*, and was soon certain that this writing concerned the three-master *Britannia*, Captain Harry Grant, out of Glasgow and which had not been heard of for more than a year.

ARABELLA: A year! How long that must seem to the poor castaways! As for me, if I were living for a year in such conditions, I would be dead at the end of a week! Continue, my nephew!

GLENARVAN: If one knew the name of the ship, unfortunately one didn't know at what point in the South Seas it had shipwrecked. It was indeed from the latitude a question of the Australian areas—but as for the longitude—

ARABELLA: Oh, don't mention those scientific words! Longitude! Latitude! That makes my head spin and gets on my nerves! And then, my nephew, you left for London?

GLENARVAN: Dear aunt, yes, but before doing I sent a telegram to the newspapers thus conceived: "For information as to the fate of the three-master *Britannia* out of Glasgow, address Lord Glenarvan, Castle Malcolm, Dumbarton County, Scotland." Let's hope that this note will be read by some member of the family of Captain Grant. (returns the bottle to Mulray)

ARABELLA: Let's hope, rather, that this poor Captain has neither wife nor children that his disappearance will have reduced to despair!

MULRAY: (aside) The little Miss is very nervous—but she has a good heart.

ARABELLA: Finally, my nephew, what are you going to do?

GLENARVAN: I am going to attempt to interest the Admiralty in the fate of the castaways. England will not hesitate to come to the aid of some of its children lost on a desert island!

ARABELLA: This story moved me, exhausted me! I am not accustomed to submit to such emotions. Replace this bottle on the table, Mulray. I cannot see it any longer. It seems to me that these poor castaways are going to emerge from it living—to implore us! Your arm, nephew, I am going to walk a little.

GLENARVAN: Take Wilson's arm, dear auntie; as for me, I am going to Glasgow. I must have a reply, it must be favorable, or if not the Admiralty had best watch out. (coming back) In an hour I'll be back. Till later, Wilson.

ARABELLA: (moving away leaning on Wilson's arm) Gently, quite gently, Captain Wilson. (stopping) Ah! Mulray—

MULRAY: Milady?

ARABELLA: You will wait here for news I requested of the chamber maid.

MULRAY: Yes, Milady.

ARABELLA: Gently, Captain Wilson.

MULRAY: (watching Wilson and Arabella leave) Yes, yes, a brave and worthy Miss—but who was right not to get married. What a comical wife and mother she would make.

(Bob rushes in from the right like a man fleeing and who wishes to avoid being seen. He taps Mulray on the shoulder.)

BOB: Mulray.

MULRAY: (turning) Huh? Who goes there?

BOB: Me, cousin!

MULRAY: Bob!

BOB: Yes, it is I, but in a few moments it will no longer be I if they find me—because if they find me, they'll catch me—and if they catch me—they'll hang me!

MULRAY: They'll hang you?

BOB: And I didn't steal it, cousin.

MULRAY: What have you done?

BOB: What have I done? I? I had a violent quarrel with my spouse—and (sorrowfully) I made the poor creature drink.

MULRAY: Well, but there's no great harm in that.

BOB: It's that—I made her drink—sea water.

MULRAY: Ah!

BOB: Lots of sea water.

MULRAY: And she's very ill?

BOB: Very ill! So ill, cousin, that the unfortunate woman is resting at the bottom of the cup.

MULRAY: The cup! What cup?

BOB: The big one! The ocean.

MULRAY: Wretch! You drowned your wife!

BOB: It was in self defense, cousin. Here's the story. We were taking a boat ride in a canoe, my wife and I. You know how jealous she is of my erstwhile charms. I am young, attractive, witty, and it's not my fault if the ladies notice all that. Today, there were several who noticed it, and my spouse, as we navigated, was quarreling with me on that subject. I was seeking to calm her, when suddenly she stood up, she got carried away, seized me by the throat and started choking me, to the point of making the canoe capsize. She pushed me, I pushed her back! She clung to me, I clung to her and we rolled in the waves together. Some moments later I found myself on the shore but I found I was there alone. I looked on all sides, I searched, I called. Elmira didn't reappear! Filled with shock and drenched to the bone, I then set myself to flee, thinking I heard a terrible voice shouting at me: What have you done with your wife?

MULRAY: And what brings you here is remorse?

BOB: Yes, remorse, horrifying remorse! And fear of the constables. Ah, my friend, widowhood is perhaps very nice, but to enjoy it at your ease you must not have brought it about yourself!

MULRAY: Finally, what are you coming here to do, wretch?

BOB: I thought you wouldn't want to be the cousin of a hanged man—and that you would have me admitted aboard the *Duncan* which belongs to Lord Glenarvan and must soon depart.

MULRAY: The crew is complete, my poor Bob!

BOB: In that case, since no one knows me in this house, try to have them take me as—a servant—to do everything—even stuff I don't know.

MULRAY: All they need here is a chamber maid, and it's our cousin Rebecca who is going to occupy the place.

BOB: Cousin Rebecca? Why, no! She won't come! She's at Malcolm where she's getting married—but not a chamber maid. She's marrying!

MULRAY: Well! Lady Arabella is going to be happy. What a crisis.

BOB: You are worrying about Lady Arabella instead of me? What's going to become of me?

MULRAY: Go to Glasgow! You will find some ship ready to leave! Ah! If you need money, here's some. (giving him money)

BOB: (pocketing the money) Money! That's not what's going to console me. (holding out his hand) Have you got any more?

MULRAY: Yes, but that I need for myself, and I'm keeping it.

BOB: (aside) Egoist! (aloud) No, decidedly, I won't go to Glasgow. I must find a way— Ah! I think I've got one!

Listen, here's what I am going to do. (ringing is heard) I—someone's coming.

MULRAY: Escape, cousin.

BOB: I am escaping, but I have an idea we will see each other again soon. (leaves)

MULRAY: Poor Bob! What's he expect? Who's this coming to us?

(Robert and Mary dressed in mourning present themselves at the gate of the park. Mulray opens it for them.)

ROBERT: Lord Glenarvan, if you please.

MULRAY: His Lordship isn't here, but we are expecting his return at any minute.

ROBERT: There sis, let's stay and wait. (goes to camp himself on a chair, arms folded)

MULRAY: Well, this little fellow isn't embarrassed or lacking resolve.

MARY: No, Robert. We will come back in an hour, sir.

MULRAY: You can stay here, Miss. Besides, here's Lady Arabella, Lord Glenarvan's aunt.

ROBERT: A woman is not the same thing.

MARY: Robert.

(Enter Arabella on the arm of Wilson.)

ARABELLA: I can't stand it any more! Strolling is very tiring! This obligation of always placing one foot in front of the other.

MARY: Pardon us, Madame, but having read a notice inserted into a newspaper relative to the ship *Britannia*.

ARABELLA: Heavens! Would you be part of the unlucky family?

ROBERT: (going to her) We are the children of Captain Grant, Madame.

ARABELLA: Ah! my God! The—the children of Cap— yet again a source of violent emotions! Mulray, quick, a seat. (falls into an arm chair) The children of poor— Cap—We've—we've found him.

MARY and ROBERT: Found!!!

ARABELLA: In the belly of a shark!

ROBERT: What?

ARABELLA: The bottle—ah! Emotion disturbs my ideas.

MARY: Madame, explain yourself, I entreat you.

ARABELLA: Eh! Can I do it, agitated the way I am? That horrible beast whose name I just pronounced? Wilson, explain, I beg you. Explain.

WILSON: Right away, milady. (to Robert) You say that you are—

ROBERT: (in a determined tone) My sister Mary and I, Robert Grant, son of the brave Captain of that name. And here it is, eight months that we are without news of our father and our brother James, embarked on the Britannia! Now, in your turn, sir, tell us quickly what you know.

MARY: Please excuse the excitability of my brother. He's only fourteen.

ROBERT: Well! Fourteen! Is that nothing? Three-quarters of a man!

WILSON: Know then that three days ago we fished out of the straits a bottle in which was a document concerning the fate of the Britannia.

ROBERT: Written by my father?

WILSON: Yes!

ROBERT: I wish to see it, sir. (to Arabella) Madame! (pressing her hands) Give it to me, Madame, so that I can at least kiss his script.

MARY: Robert!

WILSON: His Lordship took this document with him to communicate it to the Lords of the Admiralty.

MARY: And what does this paper say, sir?

WILSON: It says that the *Britannia* shipwrecked and that—

ROBERT: But, my father—my brother James?

WILSON: The few words that remained legible allow us to affirm that Captain Grant and his son escaped death! Cast on an island in the South Seas. They demand help.

ROBERT: And where is this island?

WILSON: Its location is unfortunately undetermined. But some indications will allow us to attempt rescue.

ROBERT: Then, they must leave, leave as fast as possible. Right, Madame?

ARABELLA: He's charming, this dear little devil! I adore him already!

MARY: And what can be hoped, sir?

WILSON: That the Admiralty will not refuse to send a ship into the parts indicated.

MARY: (going to Wilson) But if my father—if my brother have been abandoned already in this desert isle without provisions, without clothes. Ah! pardon me, Madame. But it's more than I can stand! Tears are choking me.

ROBERT: Mary! My sister!

ARABELLA: Ah! my God! There's what—I'm bursting into tears myself. Yes, I'm bursting, I'm bursting.

WILSON: Have good hope, Miss and you, too, my young friend. Lord Glenarvan is influential. The Admiralty will not allow brave subjects of the Queen who demand assistance to perish.

(Glenarvan has appeared at the back of the stage and listened to Wilson's last words.)

GLENARVAN: The Admiralty has refused.

ROBERT and MARY: Refused!

ARABELLA: Ah! Great God!

GLENARVAN: They spoke of the millions vainly spent in the search for *Franklin*! The Admiralty declared the document obscure, unintelligible! It said that the ruin of these unfortunates was from a date so distant already, that there was no longer any chance of saving them.

ROBERT: No more hope!

MARY: My father! My poor father!

GLENARVAN: Your father! Miss....

WILSON: Yes, Milord. Mary and Robert Grant, the two children of the castaway captain.

GLENARVAN: Miss! If I had known who you were—I would have—

MARY: We thank you, Milord, for what you really tried to do. But as for me, I will not renounce saving my father and my brother. If the folks of the Admiralty are without heart and guts, the Queen is good, she's a mother, and she will understand me. I will go find the Queen!

GLENARVAN: You won't be allowed to go to Her Majesty.

ROBERT: Well, I will go wait for her in the highways. I will throw myself under the feet of her horses, and, dying though I may be when they pick me up, God will give me enough strength to shout to the Queen! Save my father and my brother.

ARABELLA: (weeping) Why, he's an angel, this little devil.

MARY: Come, Robert, let's go.

GLENARVAN: Miss—

ROBERT: Milord, allow me to see, before we go away, this document fallen into your hands, this writing—

GLENARVAN: (giving him the paper) Here it is.

ROBERT: Sis! Look at these lines that are almost effaced! Yes, it's really our father's writing! See! See! His hand did not tremble in writing.

MARY: Yes, yes, I recognize it! Oh dear and last letter of a castaway, let me cover you with my kisses and my tears!

ROBERT: (weeping) Be careful, sis, not to efface anything! Alas, some words are hardly legible as it is.

ARABELLA: (bursting into tears) Ah, my breaking heart! I can no longer stand it. I cannot. (to Glenarvan) Do you know, nephew, that this Lord of the Admiralty is a heartless man? Yes, heartless, and I am going to write him what I think of his inhuman proceedings! These poor children, what's going to become of them?

MARY: If Her Majesty refuses to listen to us, Madame— well, we—we— Ah! I don't know. I don't know. (suffocated by tears)

GLENARVAN: Have you family in Glasgow, Miss?

MARY: Our mother has been no more for a long while, alas! In departing on this expedition which ought to crown and adorn his life as a sailor, our father confided us to the care of his sister who just died, and for whom we are still in mourning! We are alone in the world, Milord!

ARABELLA: Poor children!

GLENARVAN: (aside) And this young girl is so beautiful—so charming—with no support, without defenders! (aloud) Miss, and you, my lad, hear what I am going to tell you. By writing this document and throwing it into the sea, Captain Grant confided it to God himself. And if God caused it to fall into our hands, it was because he wanted to charge us with the salvation of these unfortunate castaways.

MARY: Milord, what do you mean?

GLENARVAN: My ship is a steam yacht of 800 hundred tons. Christopher Columbus and Magellan didn't have such fine ships when they crossed the seas! With the *Duncan* I can tour the world. Well, I will go in search of Captain Grant!

MARY: (falling at Glenarvan's feet) Ah! Milord!

GLENARVAN: Rise, Miss! I am only fulfilling a duty heaven has charged me with.

ROBERT: Thanks, you are a brave and worthy man.

ARABELLA: Fine, very fine, Glenarvan!

ROBERT: But, where will you search for my father and my brother?

GLENARVAN: This document says the shipwreck took place on the 37th parallel. Well, if necessary we will trace this parallel until we locate your father! Right, Wilson?

WILSON: Yes! Your Lordship is right.

ROBERT: Milord, take me!

MARY: Robert!

ROBERT: Yes, sister! Yes! Let Milord take me on his ship if he likes, but let him take me! I feel that I will find our dear castaways!

MARY: Robert—you mean to leave me alone—alone and possibly more desperate than before? Think that I have only you in the world.

ROBERT: Mary! Mary! My sister!

GLENARVAN: Miss, the *Duncan* is a fine ship! It offers all the comforts necessary even for a long crossing. And if you think that a young girl would be able to travel in our midst without being accompanied by some other woman—I would say to you: Miss, come with your brother.

MARY: Milord, your generosity. I don't know what to reply to you, alas!

ARABELLA: (forcefully) Reply yes, Mary—and because a young girl cannot travel alone on board a ship, well—well, I will be there as well—on the trip.

MARY: You, Madame!

ROBERT: That's well! That's very well, Madame! Ah, hold on—I have to hug you. (rushes on Arabella)

ARABELLA: Hug, little one, hug! How much emotion, Lord, how much emotion! But they are good and do not cause harm. Yes, Mary, we will depart together! After all, a good ship is still better than a good carriage. That slides! You don't feel yourself moving! By the way! And Louisa, my adored parakeet! Bah! She, too, will be on the voyage.

MARY: Ah! Madame! My whole life will not suffice to prove to you my gratitude.

ARABELLA: That's all right! That's all right! Let's not get softened up any further.

GLENARVAN: (to Wilson) The *Duncan* is equipped, its crew is complete! Have it provisioned for a long campaign, and in a week we will be at sea.

WILSON: It shall be done, Milord.

(Bob, dressed in woman's clothes and disguised in a manner to complete the illusion, appears at the back.)

SERVANT: (to Arabella) Milady, Mistress Rebecca.

ARABELLA: Show her in. The new chamber-maid I was expecting.

(Bob advances and passes near Mulray.)

MULRAY: (low) Bob!

BOB: (low) There was no other way! Cousin Rebecca gave me her clothes, and—

ARABELLA: (considering her) Come closer. She has a very good figure! A little large—but a good figure! Nephew, will you allow me to question her?

GLENARVAN: At your ease, auntie dear, at your ease. (to Wilson) Are you coming, Wilson? (goes and chats with the other characters)

ARABELLA: Come closer, Mistress Rebecca. I know that you are a devoted, zealous girl—of exemplary morals.

BOB: And cousins with Mulray, who will answer for me, Milady.

MULRAY: (aside) The beast is compromising me.

ARABELLA: If you can deal with the habitual state of my nerves—if your service is attentive and kind—I think we will get along perfectly.

BOB: (in a feminine voice) I will do all that I can to please, Milady.

ARABELLA: Your face is completely sympathetic.

BOB: (coyly) Yes, yes. They often say that of me, (aside) the ladies.

ARABELLA: Your service with me will be more that of a female companion than that of a maid.

BOB: (to Mulray) I prefer that.

ARABELLA: You know how to knit and sew, I suppose?

BOB: (simpering) Certainly, Madame, I know how to sew, iron, splice, make rice. (aside) Yikes!

MULRAY: Clumsy!

ARABELLA: Make a splice—take rice—?

MULRAY: He means—no—she means—

BOB: (troubled) I mean to say—to offer—to offer a rice— fat or thin or any other object of consumption. (aside) I'm screwing myself up!

ARABELLA: I must warn you I am departing on a long voyage! You aren't afraid of being seasick?

BOB: Me? No more than a shark!

ARABELLA: (uttering a scream) Oh, never use that word—never!

BOB: (to Mulray) Once I am aboard, I'll make myself scarce.

GLENARVAN: Mulray!

MULRAY: Milord!

GLENARVAN: Call everybody!

MULRAY: Right away, milord. (leaves)

ARABELLA: And as for me, I am going to place my luggage under the surveillance of Mistress Rebecca! Soon, children! Follow me, Rebecca. Come, daughter. (leaves)

GLENARVAN: Miss, they're taking you to Glasgow where you really intend to make your preparations for departure?

MARY: Yes, milord.

(Servants and Sailors enter.)

GLENARVAN: My friends, in a week, we will again take to sea.

ALL: Ah! Ah!

GLENARVAN: This time we are going to fulfill a noble passion. It will be, perhaps, rough work, a perilous voyage. But in achieving it, we will have returned a brave father with his two children, and a brave sailor to his country. Are you ready to follow me?

ALL: Yes, yes!

ROBERT: (to Glenarvan) Ah! Milord, how I love you.

GLENARVAN: No more than I love you already, my lad! May God come to our aid, and we will find Harry Grant and his son.

ALL: Hurrah! Hurrah! Hurrah! Long live Lord Glenarvan!

CURTAIN

ACT II

Scene 3

THE YACHT *DUNCAN*

The stage represents the dining room of the yacht *Duncan*. Sumptuous furniture, wainscoting in precious woods. Arm chairs and divans. Nautical instruments. In the middle a serving table. To the right and left numbered cabins opening on the dining hall. Cabins 2 and 3 are on the same side on the left. At the rear, a rich staircase with a double, golden ramp which leads on deck, and which permits one of the yacht's masts to be seen plus its rigging. The ward room of the *Duncan* must reproduce all the luxury of English yachts.

Bob is dressed as a woman still, and is occupied shaving before a mirror. His face is entirely covered with shaving cream and he's shaving his right cheek.

BOB: Quick! Quick! That's what presses! I have to play with the razor under pain of betraying my sex! Oh! Elmira! It's you who reduced me to this cruel extremity. If you hadn't pushed me into the sea, I wouldn't have dragged you into the waves with me. You would still exist, Elmira! I wouldn't be devoured by remorse, and condemned to shave myself every two days! (shaving with frenzy) Ah! I won't be completely at peace until I've put my foot on dry land somewhere! Good—one side is shaved! Now to the other. (begins to shave his left cheek) If Lady Arabella saw me in such a later—what a crisis! (a bell rings) Son of a sea-horse! It's she! And I've only one side done!

ARABELLA: (emerging from Cabin) Well! Rebecca?

BOB: I'm here, I'm here, Milady.

(Bob hides his razor and presents himself so that only the shaved cheek can be seen and not the lathered side.)

ARABELLA: I rang, my girl.

BOB: I was running. I was in the process of twisting the windlass. Yie! And of arranging milady's trunks. They've been placed in her cabin—in #4, yesterday evening, when we embarked.

ARABELLA: That's fine. (passing to the other side) Have you seen Robert and Mary this morning?

BOB: (changing position to hide the lather on his face) Brother and sister are above, on deck leaning on the bulwarks.

ARABELLA: Bulwarks?

BOB: It's a nautical term my cousin Mulray taught me.

ARABELLA: Very good. Has my paper arrived?

BOB: Paper?

ARABELLA: Yes. *The Illustrated London News.*

BOB: Milady expects to receive her newspaper—in the middle of the ocean?

ARABELLA: That's true. I was forgetting. (going up) I am going above to take the air. Ah! (coming back down on the unshaven side of Bob) I feel a little giddy! Give me your arm to the staircase.

BOB: (turning to the other side) My—my arm? Here, Milady, here. (offers it to her)

ARABELLA: No—not that one; the other one.

(Arabella moves to his unshaven side.)

BOB: Here, here, Milady.

ARABELLA: But, why are you changing sides like this?

BOB: Wh—why, milady? (at this moment a loud bell) Ah, they are ringing, milady, they are ringing. (pointing to Cabin #3) One would say it is coming from this cabin.

ARABELLA: But that cabin cannot be occupied! Aren't my nephew and Captain Wilson on the bridge?

BOB: On the contrary, I saw them there. (a new and more violent ringing than the first. (heading toward cabin number 3) I have to see! I have....

(Bob rapidly wipes his cheek.)

ARABELLA: Just think of it, Rebecca! If someone of the male sex were found there?

BOB: (forgetting) That wouldn't bother me much!

ARABELLA: (shocked) Huh? What?

BOB: (getting uneasy) No, I meant to say—that it wouldn't please me. (aside) Satanic shirts! I keep forgetting that Mistress Rebecca is in there.

(Third ringing—and the door of cabin 3 opens. A head peers out with a night cap on. This head wears glasses that are never put on the eyes but on the nose.)

ARABELLA: Great God! What's that?

(Arabella flees to the other side of the room.)

PAGANEL: (in a bath robe/dressing gown) Waiter! Waiter!

BOB: A man!

PAGANEL: (emerging from the cabin) Well—service is given in a very funny way on this steamboat! They make you pay enough for the passage.

ARABELLA: Who is this monster?

PAGANEL: (noticing Arabella) Ah, passengers. (raises his cotton night cap and bows) Madame. (to Bob) Miss.

BOB: (curtsying) Sir!

PAGANEL: I ask your pardon for presenting myself in this gear! Imagine, ladies, that I rang three times, called twice, and that not one servant bothered himself. I pay my compliments to the Cunard Company! I would have done better to take a French Transatlantic.

ARABELLA: (to Bob) But, this gentleman is mad. We must inform the authorities.

PAGANEL: It's like last night! Impossible to sleep! I arrived yesterday evening at Glasgow, exhausted by thirty hours of voyage. I went to bed. What do I hear in the cabin next to number 2? (points to the cabin)

ARABELLA: (aside) Mine! What did this gentleman hear?

PAGANEL: Formidable snoring, ladies!

ARABELLA: (scandalized) Snoring.

PAGANEL: There's no doubt about it, it was an old gentleman.

ARABELLA: An old gentleman! (carried away) But it's I, sir, who occupy this cabin!

PAGANEL: What, Madame! The old gentleman was you! (confused)

ARABELLA: Snoring! Ah! Ah! Rebecca? I feel ill. Salts, my flask! Snoring!

PAGANEL: Pardon, a thousand pardons, Madame—from the moment it's a question of you—it wasn't snoring— it was sighing—very tender sighing.

ARABELLA: Ah! Ah! My nervous attack! My nervous attack!

BOB: Her nervous attach! She's having her nervous attack. (slaps Arabella's hands)

PAGANEL: Her—her attack! What to do?

BOB: Quick—a glass of water and pour vinegar on this handkerchief.

PAGANEL: Here, here, miss!

(Paganel pours water from a carafe on his handkerchief.)

PAGANEL: Let her breathe this. (handing the handkerchief)

BOB: Something to drink now, something to drink.

PAGANEL: To drink? Yes! Right away. (pours the flask of vinegar in a cup) Make her drink this! Poor lady! And I am the cause.

ARABELLA: (drinking) Yuck! Fie! Horror! What's this?

PAGANEL: Water! A glass of fresh water that I poured for you, beautiful lady.

ARABELLA: Why, it's vinegar.

BOB: It's the flask of vinegar.

PAGANEL: It's the flask! Heavens! Ah! Pardon, a thousand pardons, Madame! It's a distraction.

(The clock sounds on deck.)

BOB: Good! The lunch clock.

PAGANEL: The devil! I've only got time to finish dressing! Deign to excuse me, Madame, I affirm what I want to say: sighs—mere sighs—where did I put my nightcap? (noticing it on a chair where a woman's hat is also seen) Ah! There it is. (going to take it and turning to Arabella) Simple sighs, Madame. (takes the woman's hat without looking and bows) Madame, I have indeed the honor

ARABELLA: My hat! That's my hat, sir.

PAGANEL: Your? Goodness, it's true. (placing it down) That makes two distractions! That's astonishing, Madame, as for me, I never get distracted! They were sighs, Madame, tender sighs. (goes back into his cabin)

ARABELLA: But, who is this man?

(Glenarvan enters.)

ARABELLA: Ah! My nephew!

GLENARVAN: My dear aunt, Robert and Mary, not yet being ready, beg you to dine without them.

ARABELLA: Fine, fine. Tell me, Glenarvan, why didn't you forewarn me that you were bringing a stranger, that you lodged him precisely in the cabin next to mine? How shocking this is. (pointing to the cabin) That one there!

GLENARVAN: I don't understand.

WILSON: A stranger in this cabin?

ARABELLA: Ask Rebecca! He's a horrible man.

BOB: Horrible! It's quite true!

GLENARVAN: Some intruder, no question! We are indeed going to see.

(Glenarvan heads towards cabin #3. Paganel appears in travel costume.)

PAGANEL: (gaily) Ah! Ah! The passengers are gathering for lunch! That's lucky! But here, it's like a table *d'hôte*! Each for himself. The best place and the choicest tidbits. Eh! Eh!

(Paganel tours around the table and at last chooses his place next to Arabella.)

ARABELLA: (indignant) Be gone! Be gone!

PAGANEL: (aside) The Snorer.

GLENARVAN: (to Wilson) Ah, indeed! Will you explain to me, Captain?

PAGANEL: The Captain….

WILSON: Why, milord, I don't know. I don't understand.

PAGANEL: It's necessary that I pay my respects to him. (going to Wilson) Captain, allow me to shake your hand. Yesterday evening the fog was so thick that I didn't even notice you. The porter placed my luggage in this cabin that I had retained hurriedly, on board the *Scotia*, and I nestled right in it. Captain Barton, I am very happy to enter into relations with you.

GLENARVAN: (aside) Great! He's a passenger who mistook his ship!

PAGANEL: But let's not make these ladies wait. (offers his arm to Arabella) Deign to accept, Madame.

ARABELLA: (avoiding him, proudly) I am not accepting anything from you, sir.

PAGANEL: (aside) Not polite, the snorer!

GLENARVAN: (aside) This brave gentleman has the manner of a proud character! Look, Wilson, let's present ourselves. We must at least know with whom we are dealing!

WILSON: (to Paganel) Sir, will you allow me to present to you, his Lordship—Lord Glenarvan?

PAGANEL: (bowing) Ah! Milord, enchanted to make your acquaintance.

ARABELLA: (aside) As for me, I am not enchanted to have made his!

PAGANEL: (confidentially) I warn you, Milord, that we have here (pointing to Arabella) a traveling companion—of a very annoying—nervosity.

GLENARVAN: (smiling) She's my aunt, sir!

PAGANEL: Huh? Your— (aside) The Devil!

GLENARVAN: (presenting Arabella to him) Lady Arabella Glenarvan.

PAGANEL: Milady, certainly—I—I am (pointing to Bob). Miss is your daughter, no doubt? Fine bearing.

ARABELLA: My—my daughter! My chamber-maid, sir!

PAGANEL: (aside) I don't have a lucky tongue today.

GLENARVAN: But, you, sir—?

PAGANEL: Ah! Milord, I ask your pardon for presenting myself but, at sea one can be more easy about etiquette!

GLENARVAN: To whom have I the honor of speaking, sir?

PAGANEL: Jacques-Eliaun-Jean-Marie Paganel.

GLENARVAN: Paganel! You are Mr. Paganel?

PAGANEL: Perpetual Secretary of the Paris Geographic Society, corresponding member of the societies of Bombay, Leipzig, London, St. Petersburg, and headed to India to gather there the works of the great travelers.

GLENARVAN: Mr. Paganel, I can only congratulate myself on meeting on board one of the most distinguished scientists of France. (aside to Wilson) And the most distracted of men!

WILSON: Everything's explained then.

ARABELLA: (to Glenarvan) Is he going to dine with us?

GLENARVAN: (low) My dear auntie, he must be dying of hunger. Let him regain his strength before informing him of where he is and where he's going.

(All except Bob take their places around the table. Paganel finds himself next to Arabella who is furious.)

GLENARVAN: And now, Mr. Paganel, would you allow me to address a question to you?

PAGANEL: Why, of course! Twenty questions, milord, thirty questions—as many questions as you like.

GLENARVAN: Once arrived in India, have you chosen Calcutta as the point of departure for your travels?

PAGANEL: Yes, milord! I will launch myself from Calcutta to see India. My most beautiful dream is going to be realized in the country of elephants and thugs.

ARABELLA: (holding out her glass) Sugar. I'd like some sugar in my tea.

PAGANEL: Here, milady, here. Conceive, milord (pouring salt in Arabella's tea as he speaks)

ARABELLA: Why, that's salt, sir, that's salt!

PAGANEL: Ah, pardon! Ah, yes, it's salt. Yet another distraction! It's astounding. I who never get dis—

GLENARVAN: (passing the sugar bowl) Here's the sugar.

PAGANEL: Thanks, I don't take any.

GLENARVAN: It's for my aunt!

(Paganel pours the sugar bowl into Arabella's cup.)

ARABELLA: What are you doing?

PAGANEL: I am desolated, Madame, but it won't come out! It's broken! (to Glenarvan) I am entrusted, Milord, with fulfilling an important mission. It's a question of running along the northeast base of the Himalayas and determining at last if the Irrawaddy is joined at Bramapoutri in the northeast of Assam.

ARABELLA: (aside) What terrifying words this geographer has in his mouth.

GLENARVAN: Mr. Paganel, I don't wish to prolong your mistake any longer! Know that you are turning your back on the Indian peninsula.

PAGANEL: Huh? What? You mean the *Scotia*?

WILSON: This ship is not the *Scotia*!

PAGANEL: It's not the *Scotia*?

WILSON: It's the *Duncan*, the pleasure yacht of his Lordship, Lord Glenarvan.

PAGANEL: (uttering a scream) The *Duncan*! A pleasure yacht! Oh, great God! Stop—then—stop—the bell—the bell— (pulls forcefully on one of the long tresses hanging from Arabella's back) Stop! Stop!

ARABELLA: (uttering a scream) Ah! The wretch. Those are my tresses, sir!

PAGANEL: Receive my excuses. I actually was saying to myself—they don't ring!

(All rise from the table.)

PAGANEL: (running like a mad man) But I have to stop the *Duncan*. They've got to land me.

ARABELLA: (beside herself) Yes, debark him—and then throw him into the sea.

GLENARVAN: Arabella! Auntie! (to Paganel) Sir, it's impossible to debark you.

WILSON: We're more than a hundred miles from the coast.

PAGANEL: In that case, a canoe! A canoe! Let them row me to land.

WILSON: Calm down.

PAGANEL: The *Duncan*! And where's the *Duncan* going?

GLENARVAN: To South America.

PAGANEL: (tearing his hair) South America! What will the Paris Geographic Society say? To take one ship for another! To awaken on route to South American, when I thought I was leaving for the Indies! Ah, it's enough to make you tear (continues to tear his hair).

BOB: (to Paganel) Take care, sir, you don't have much already!

PAGANEL: (to Glenarvan) It's true! Ah! What an idea! Milord, there's a way to fix everything.

GLENARVAN: What way is that?

PAGANEL: India's a fine country! It affords travelers marvelous surprises! Wells the steersman need only give a turn of the wheel, and the *Duncan* just as easily heads towards Calcutta as—since it's a pleasure voyage!

ROBERT: (entering with Mary) A pleasure trip.

GLENARVAN: Sir, the *Duncan* is en route to seek poor castaways.

PAGANEL: Castaways?

MARY: Castaways of the *Britannia*, sir, and among them—

ROBERT: And among them both our father and brother!

MARY: We are the children of Captain Grant—

PAGANEL: Captain Grant! That heroic sailor who is rushing to discover the South Pole?

ROBERT: Himself.

GLENARVAN: You understand, sir, we don't have the right to lose an hour.

MULRAY: (entering from the rear) Captain!

WILSON: What's wrong?

MULRAY: A ship is in sight, heading straight for us!

WILSON: What ship is it?

MULRAY: The *Saint Laurent,* a transatlantic en route to France.

PAGANEL: Milord, this is an act of heaven! You are going to have me transferred.

GLENARVAN: As you please, sir.

ARABELLA: (to Bob) I won't be the one to regret this geographer!

BOB: (aside) It suits me well enough!

WILSON: (to Mulray) Signal the liner that we wish to communicate with it.

MULRAY: Right, Captain.

PAGANEL: At the same time, my friend, make them take up my luggage which is placed in that cabin. (points to cabin #9, in which Arabella's luggage has been provisionally placed)

(Mulray leaves and sailors come to remove the trunks as the conversation continues.)

MULRAY: Yes, sir.

PAGANEL: (to Glenarvan) Good! I'm saved! Milord, above all, allow me to say to you that's it's a noble action, going in search of castaways. It's great, it's generous—it's—but may I know how you've been led to fly to the rescue of these unfortunates?

GLENARVAN: By our finding a document at sea.

PAGANEL: A document! Why it's an envoy from Providence!

GLENARVAN: That's the way we looked at it.

PAGANEL: Could I see this document? It interests me to the highest degree.

GLENARVAN: Nothing could be simpler.

(Glenarvan gives the document to Paganel.)

PAGANEL: Ah! this note is really in bad condition! The sea did not respect it?

ROBERT: Why, yes, sir! You can still read it very well!

PAGANEL: Indeed, there remain some words. (reading) Captain Grant and his son—Bal—Austral—*Britannia*—at 37° longitude—again—help—they are lost! (speaking) Thirty-seven degrees latitude—the longitude is unfortunately lacking! But in that case, where are you going to direct your search?

GLENARVAN: Precisely on the 37th parallel—south.

PAGANEL: Fine—very fine—but I think wait a bit—yes—yes—ah! My friends—gang—there's a fragmentary line that clarifies this document completely.

GLENARVAN: Which one?

ROBERT: Speak—speak, sir!

MARY: Sir, it's a question of our father.

ARABELLA: (to Paganel who is absorbed in his thoughts) Why, speak, won't you? This is giving us emotions! This geographer will be the death of me!

PAGANEL: Yes, there's not the least doubt! G o - go - n - ce - nie gonie. The *Duncan* needn't take the trouble of following the entire 37th parallel! Gonie! It's evident that the Britannia was lost off the cost of Gonia. It's lacking "Pater"! It's in Patagonia you must search for the castaways.

GLENARVAN: Yes—yes—he's right! It cannot be more clear! In Patagonia! And we didn't understand. Ah! Sir, meeting you on board the *Duncan* is truly providential!

PAGANEL: And this document is so explicit that I will be able to find them with my eyes completely closed.

WILSON: Still, if Captain Grant lost his ship on the coast of Patagonia, why hasn't he been able to repatriate himself yet, by reaching Buenos Aires or Montevideo?

PAGANEL: And if he was made a prisoner by the indigenous, sir? If he was taken into the interior of the land, as happened to one of my compatriots who remained thirty-two years in the hands of the Patagons! Yes, the shipwreck took place on the coast situated on the east of Patagonia. Taken captive, the shipwrecks crossed the Cordilleras. They have scaled the hell of Antero and come down in the Pampas to stop at the foot where there are forts that the great rivers bathe. It's there, that's where they are, that's where they are waiting for us, that's where they are calling us! I hear them! I see them, I see them! Hope friends, hope we are racing to you! We are racing to—

MARY: (weeping) Ah! sir, sir!

PAGANEL: I was already in Patagonia! Courage, Miss, courage. You will see them again!

ROBERT: But, if, as you say, they were taken in the interior, how were they able to throw this bottle into the sea?

PAGANEL: How? Nothing could be simpler, my friend. Wasn't Captain Grant able to throw this bottle into a stream and that stream took it to the ocean?

MARY: That's true, sir.

GLENARVAN: Decidedly, Mr. Paganel is right. There's no possible objection.

MULRAY: (entering) We are in communication with the *Saint Laurent*.

PAGANEL: Fine! Put my luggage on board.

ROBERT: What—you still intend to leave—to leave us?

PAGANEL: Surely.

ROBERT: Come off it! Are you capable of doing it?

PAGANEL: Yes, I am capable of it.

MARY: My brother's right, sir. You affirmed that you would go to the place of shipwreck, eyes shut! For pity, do not abandon us, and do not leave us, sir!

PAGANEL: Miss—certainly—I would—but it's imposs—

ROBERT: I beg you, sir, I entreat you! (grasping Paganel by his coat) Anyway, I won't let you go.

PAGANEL: What! What, young man!

ROBERT: No, sir, no, no! I'm attaching myself to you!

PAGANEL: But my mission, children, my mission?

ROBERT: You are an honest man, sir, and your first mission is to help the unfortunate—who are dying, perhaps!

PAGANEL: (to Glenarvan) What he says is true enough.

GLENARVAN: Yes, certainly, and the Bramapoutri can wait.

ROBERT: It will wait, sir.

PAGANEL: (hesitating) It's certain that it won't go anywhere—the Bramapoutri.

GLENARVAN: Consider, also that in this work you will have the right to associate the name of France with that of England, and what is much finer—to put science in the service of humanity!

ARABELLA: (moved) Ah! How well said that is—to the degree that I, who do not care for your company—well, I ask you to remain, Mr. Geographer.

PAGANEL: Certainly, milady, an invitation so graciously formulated—

GLENARVAN: Believe me, sir, let Providence act. It sent us this document and we embarked. It threw you aboard the *Duncan*—and you shan't leave.

ALL: Yes, sir, yes!

PAGANEL: Well?

MULRAY: (shouting through his bullhorn) The *Saint Laurent* is going to continue on its journey.

PAGANEL: Well, let the *Saint Laurent* leave us alone!

ALL: Ah! You are staying.

PAGANEL: I am staying, and I reply to you we are going to do things promptly.

(A whistle indicates the departure of the *Saint Laurent*.)

MARY: Ah, sir, accept all the gratitude of the castaways.

ROBERT: Your hand, Mr. Paganel. (grasps it) No, better than that. (jumps on his neck)

PAGANEL: (shaken) What a rough little man! He's a young lion!

ARABELLA: (moved, going to Paganel) Sir, I pardon you—for the salt poured in my tea, for the vinegar I drank. Continue to act as you are doing. I will forgive you for the rest.

PAGANEL: Thanks a lot, milord— (catching himself) Milady. Ah, great God!

ARABELLA: (starting) What's wrong?

PAGANEL: My luggage has been put on the *Saint Laurent* and it's gone.

ARABELLA: Ah! (gaily) Now that's really a distraction. Ah! ah! ah!

PAGANEL: (running to Cabin #3) Eh! no, God be thanked. There they are.

WILSON: Then whose did we just carry up?

BOB: (going to Cabin #4) Ah! Lord God! They took them from here on a sign from Mr. Paganel.

WILSON: And they were—

BOB: Lady Arabella's luggage!

ARABELLA: (swooning) Ah! My luggage! My luggage! Now here I am without clothes and without linen. My luggage! He had them carried off. (rising abruptly and going to Paganel) I withdraw my forgiveness, sir, and I promise you a Caribbean hatred!

PAGANEL: What an unfortunate distraction I've had. I, who never get distracted.

CURTAIN

ACT II

Scene 4

THE HILL OF ANTURO

The stage represents a peak in the Cordilleras of South America. To the left, climbable mountains. To the right, a high rock which dominates the stage. In the back, a picturesque heap of mountains.

The characters, Glenarvan, Paganel, Robert, and Mulray, are dressed in ponchos and traditional costumes of the land. Glenarvan carries a rifle in a bandolier. All arrive from the right and stop.

MULETEER: Here's the peak of Anturo, which allows travelers to pass from the other side of the chain.

PAGANEL: Yes, at 6,000 feet in the air? Huh, my dear companions, what a picturesque country it is here, formed by the border of Patagonia and the Argentine Republic.

GLENARVAN: So picturesque, Mr. Paganel, that I am almost regretting that Lady Arabella and Mary Grant wanted to follow us on this voyage. They were made to remain aboard the *Duncan* which is going to wait for us on the Western littoral. That must have spared them many exhaustions.

PAGANEL: No question, but they wanted to be there when we find the castaways of the *Britannia* and that's quite natural.

GLENARVAN: Until now heaven has not granted them that joy! Here we are almost reaching the occidental side of Patagonia and nothing! Not one clue can put us on the track of the shipwrecks!

PAGANEL: All is not yet said and in the hundred thousands which remain to the cross—

MULETEER: Silence!

GLENARVAN: What's the matter?

MULETEER: Wait.

(The Muleteer rests his ear against the ground. A dull rumbling is heard.)

PAGANEL: What is it? Could it by chance be—?

MULETEER: Just now, didn't you see a flight of Pelicans fleeing?

PAGANEL: Pursued no doubt by some savage animals?

MULETEER: That's not it.

GLENARVAN: Then what is it?

(New rumblings.)

MULETEER: I hear a dull rumbling. Here, under our feet. Perhaps it's the announcement of an earthquake.

GLENARVAN: In that case, let's try to reach the other side of the mountain.

ALL: Before—

GLENARVAN: (to Muleteer) But as I think of it, we've left our little troop at a quarter of a mile—encamped, with the purpose of exploring this peak. Is there any danger for Lady Arabella and Miss Grant?

MULETEER: No! Your companions are indeed sheltered there! The peril is here!

MULRAY: If your Lordship cares to believe me, we will hasten to see if this pass of Anturo is open.

GLENARVAN: Lead the mules.

MULETEER: The peak can only be crossed on foot.

PAGANEL: It's only an affair of two or three miles.

GLENARVAN: But on the other side?

MULETEER: You will find horses to cross the Pampas. Only in passing this chain, beware of avalanches or earthquakes! These subterranean tremors, I repeat to you, are not a good omen.

PAGANEL: These cataclysms are the beauty of this country. Here the mountains move as if by enchantment. As for me, I would not be sorry to see an earthquake.

MULETEER: May heaven protect you from it, sir, and if I have advice to give you, move quickly, once you are entered into the pass, and speak only in low voices! The least noise can provoke an avalanche.

GLENARVAN: In that case, no distractions, Mr. Paganel.

PAGANEL: Distractions! Me? I never have any.

GLENARVAN: (to Muleteer) You can guide us to the summit of the pass?

MULETEER: That's outside our agreement, but there's danger. I'll remain with you.

GLENARVAN: Fine! Your time and your trouble will be amply paid.

(New rumblings.)

MULETEER: In that case, follow me. (stopping) Listen! Those rumblings are spreading through the chain! Perhaps it will be prudent to postpone—

GLENARVAN: We haven't the time to be so prudent, my friend. En route!

(All, Muleteer in the lead, scale the rocks on the left.)

PAGANEL: Useless for this Muleteer to talk. This is charming!

MULETEER: I am going to assure myself of the condition of this path. Wait here!

(As soon as Glenarvan and his companions reach the top of the rock, a terrible noise can be heard. The slope that the travelers are climbing suddenly collapses and they are hurled into the abyss at the foot of the slope.)

MULRAY: What a clubbing, Mr. Geographer!

PAGANEL: Here I am, my friend, don't be uneasy. I am not wounded—but I've lost my spectacles. (looking around him) Where are they then?

GLENARVAN: (reappearing) None of us injured? Well, and Robert? Where is Robert?

PAGANEL: I don't see him.

GLENARVAN: (calling) Robert!

ALL: Robert! Robert!

GLENARVAN: He's not answering, and in this precipice into which we ourselves were thrown, I don't see him.

PAGANEL: Perhaps the unlucky child rolled to the bottom.

MULRAY: Wait, I am going to go down there.

MULETEER: A few yards from here the slope is too steep for it to be possible. Stop, if you slip, it's death.

GLENARVAN: Anyway, I'm going there!

MULRAY: Milord, you don't have the right to expose yourself. I'm going there. But I have a wife and child — I have nothing more to say to you! Goodbye.

(Mulray descends the gulf. New rumblings are heard.)

MULETEER: Listen! The noise is increasing. The ground is shaking under our feet, more violently still! We must flee. Go back down in haste.

GLENARVAN: Flee without having found Robert—
never!

MARY: Robert—find Robert you said. Where is my
brother?

GLENARVAN: Miss, Robert—

(A huge bird appears at the left and descends obliquely into the abyss.)

MARY: (very agitated) Yes, yes. I heard your shouts re-
peated by the echo of these mountains? And I ran and I
ask you again: Where is Robert? Where is he? Where is
my brother?

GLENARVAN: Like us, no doubt, he was hurled into this
abyss.

MARY: (going to look) There! My brother! My brother!
Ah! I want to die with him.

GLENARVAN: We will save him, Miss Mary. We will
save him! Mulray has descended to search for him.

MARY: No! Let me! Let me.

(The bird reappears holding Robert in its claws—rising
slowly.)

MARY: Ah! Look, there! There—Robert!

GLENARVAN: Great God!

(Glenarvan seizes his rifle and aims at the bird.)

MARY: (on her knees) My God! Have pity! Have pity!

(A Patagonian, in national costume appears at the summit of a rock and shoulders his long carbine. The shot fires, and the bird, still holding Robert, slowly falls behind the rock. Glenarvan goes down into the gulf to search for Robert.)

MARY: Have you had compassion, My God; or must a last despair tear apart my heard? Robert! Robert!

(Glenarvan reappears carrying a fainted Robert in his arms and places him on a rock.)

MARY: Look, look, that livid pallor, and his eyes remain shut. My brother! My brother!

(Mary raises Robert's head and covers it with kisses and tears.)

PAGANEL: Wait, Miss Mary, wait! I have Lady Arabella's flask, which through distraction, I took for my snuff box. (making Robert breathe the flask) Look, look—his cheeks are beginning to show some color!

MARY: (with joy) Yes, yes—

GLENARVAN: He's coming to.

ROBERT: Mary—Sis—Ah! What a dream. (in a weak voice) What a terrible dream.

MARY: (pointing to the Patagonian) Robert, there's the man you owe your life to!

THALCAVE: No! The great spirit supported my arm and directed my weapon.

ROBERT: (holding out his hand to Thalcave) My friend, my savior, who are you?

THALCAVE: Thalcave! Born in this land, I have often escorted travelers through the defiles of our mountains.

PAGANEL: A Patagonian! I have seen a real Patagonian.

GLENARVAN: Friend, what do you ask for having saved this child? We are searching for his father, a prisoner of one of your tribes.

THALCAVE: There are no prisoners amongst us.

GLENARVAN: What! A year ago, wasn't there a ship-wreck on your coast?

THALCAVE: No shipwreck has taken place on our shores. No castaways are among my people.

MARY: My God! In that case all hope is lost!

ROBERT: Remember, friend, remember. It's my father and my brother that my sister and I are seeking!

THALCAVE: Down there, in Valparaiso, perhaps some news can be found?

ROBERT: (to Glenarvan) To Valparaiso, milord.

GLENARVAN: We are going to go there, Robert, and if we don't find new clues, we will start out all over to accomplish our mission! (to Thalcave) Friend, you can be useful, you can gather information which might escape us. Will you come with us to Valparaiso?

THALCAVE: (looking at Robert) To there and even further if necessary. The child called me his savior! (placing his hand on Robert's shoulder) He's almost my child to me. I won't leave him until the day I've delivered him into the arms of his true father!

GLENARVAN: Come on, let's continue on our way.

(New rumblings more violent than before.)

MULETEER: It's too late! Don't anyone budge!

CURTAIN

ACT II

Scene 5

THE EARTHQUAKE

The rumblings increase, and the tops of mountains collapse on every side. Heaven is on fire. A violent storm bursts. Night comes on. All the characters in consternation fall on their knees and huddle against each other.

CURTAIN

ACT III

Scene 6

A POSADA

The stage represents a hotel arranged in the manner of a Spanish posada. Side doors. Door at the rear; wooden gallery reached by a stairway which descends to the right. Doors on the gallery which open on various rooms. Chimney to the left. Tables, wooden armchairs.

FORSTER: Well, what news, Ayrton?

AYRTON: I'm coming from the coast where I left some of our companions. There I saw crossing, running and tacking—a superb ship, a steam yacht of more than eight hundred tons, which would have no trouble making twelve miles an hour! It's named the *Duncan*. It has four comrades on its bridge. It must be a pleasure yacht which can defy the fastest runners of the English fleet. Ah, if we had such a boat under our feet, comrades, we would be kings of the sea.

DICK: Is there no way for us to seize it?

AYRTON: Oh! If this *Duncan* instead of being on the roadstead of Valparaiso were on the Australian coast!

FORSTER: Yes, but this ship is not in Australia, it's in Valparaiso and we can do nothing!

AYRTON: Nothing? Perhaps!

DICK: What do you mean?

AYRTON: Listen to me carefully. The Gold feasts the Chilean miners are giving today will take place in the grand square of Valparaiso, across from the governor's palace. All the people of the town, all the sailors in the port, run in crowds to these celebrations. Like all the other ships the *Duncan* will be almost abandoned for an hour at least, and then some few determined and clever men would suffice to seize it and make it reach the sea!

FORSTER: And the *Duncan* will be ours!

AYRTON: Oh! The success of this plan would be more certain if I were able to get myself admitted on that ship, like a castaway demanding to be repatriated, or as a second mate! I could then receive you aboard during the tumult of the celebration and we would voyage to Australia, where Ayrton would become Ben-Joyce, again, supreme leader of convicts, and form his crew of his bravest companions.

DICK: We could then sail as masters of the ocean.

AYRTON: All the merchant ships would become our tributaries!

FORSTER: And I wouldn't be annoyed, for my part, to push even to Balker Island.

AYRTON: Are you mad?

FORSTER: No! I would like to know what the end was of those we abandoned there, Captain Grant, his son James, and—

AYRTON: And Burke, that ferocious beast we left with them! If he didn't kill them straight off—two winters in that desert of ice must have finished them all off.

DICK: All the same, I, too, would like to know—

BOB: (off) Innkeeper?

AYRTON: Silence!

BOB: Hey! Innkeeper! Innkeeper.

(Bob is still dressed as a woman.)

INNKEEPER: (entering) Here! Here, sir.

BOB: (resuming his feminine voice) What do you mean, "sir"? Insolent!

INNKEEPER: Excuse me, Miss, but every time I hear you without seeing you, I take you for a man.

BOB: (coyly) But, when you see me—

INNKEEPER: Oh! When I see you. (looks at him)

BOB: (turning away) The devil! I mustn't let myself be looked at this morning! I lost my razor—and for two days it's been growing—growing.

INNKEEPER: What is it you wish, miss?

BOB: The tea for Lord Glenarvan and his company.

AYRTON: (low) Glenarvan! Eh, why, he's the owner of the *Duncan*! Pay attention!

INNKEEPER: (who's gone to inspect the table) Well, you see, everything is ready! All that has to be done is to serve it when the order is given.

BOB: (aside) If I don't find a way to shave, I am lost! I cannot go to a barber in the town like— How to get my razor cleverly replaced? (aloud) Ah! My friend!

INNKEEPER: Sir—miss.

BOB: My good friend, couldn't you loan me—for a moment, something—whatever it might be?

INNKEEPER: Something, miss?

BOB: Something that cuts—

INNKEEPER: A knife?

BOB: No, something sharper. Something very sharp.

INNKEEPER: Very sharp. Ah, hold on, I have the thing for you. (goes to the back) I have the thing for you!

BOB: Bravo, I am saved!

INNKEEPER: (returning with a scythe which he finds in a corner and plants before Bob) Here!

BOB: (with terror) Huh! A scythe! What do you want me to do with that?

INNKEEPER: Why, it's very sharp! Won't it serve for the work in question?

BOB: For the work in? Never! (aside) So the wretch wants to decapitate me!

(Glenarvan, giving his arm to Mary, and Paganel, respectfully escorting Arabella, enter.)

GLENARVAN: Have us served, Mr. Innkeeper.

INNKEEPER: Right away, your Lordship. (leaves)

AYRTON: (low) The lord in question.

MARY: (sadly) Milord hasn't received any information since our arrival in Valparaiso?

GLENARVAN: None, alas!

ARABELLA: So many wearisome things, so many violent emotions, and all this to no purpose on the chimerical direction of Mr. Geographer.

(They sit down to eat. Two waiters enter and serve the tea.)

PAGANEL: Don't overwhelm me, milady, I am ceaselessly torturing myself to find a meaning in this document.

ARABELLA: And nothing?

PAGANEL: Nothing. (reading) "Captain Grant and his son."

(Ayrton and the others are startled.)

AYRTON: (low) What's he saying?

PAGANEL: (still reading) "Bal—Austral—*Britannia*—"

AYRTON: It really is a about him! Let's listen!

PAGANEL: (still reading) "*Britannia*—Austral—Bal—"

(Wilson, Thalcave, and Robert enter.)

GLENARVAN: Well, my friends?

WILSON: Nothing, milord, no clue!

MARY: Nothing.

WILSON: I have perused all the marine registers with the greatest care.

ROBERT: I've questioned all the employees, all the sailors.

THALCAVE: I've seen all those of my brothers who have left our forests and pampas to come trade in this country.

ROBERT: And no one has been able to give us a single word of hope!

MARY: My father! My poor brother!

FORSTER: (aside) The daughter of Captain Grant?

MARY: Alas, all is over!

GLENARVAN: Don't despair, Miss Mary, I will search all the shores of the Australian Ocean, I will visit each island, each sand bar, I will restore your father to you, or I will die trying.

DICK: (low) It's not good here for us. Let's leave!

AYRTON: Stay put!

PAGANEL: (reading aside) Bal—what's that word mean, bal? And agon—agon—If it's not Patagonia, then what is it?

ROBERT: Well, Milord, since we no longer have any hope of finding our beloved castaways here—let's not stay here any longer—I entreat you!

PAGANEL: Agon—agon!

ROBERT: Think of their suffering, of their despair, and this long, cruel agony which is killing them.

PAGANEL: (leaping up and rapping on the document) Agony—yes, that's it. Agony, it's the end of the word agon-, and the country, the shore, the island where they are to be found must be the beginning of the world which begins by that syllable Bal—bal.

DICK: (low) Balker! He's going to find it.

FORSTER: All is lost.

AYRTON: Silence. (aloud, rising and coming forward) Milord, praise God and thank him for leading me here that I might hear you! If Captain Harry Grant is still living, he's living on Australian earth.

(General consternation. Thalcave rises and comes forward.)

PAGANEL: Austral—that means Australia.

GLENARVAN: Who are you to speak like this?

AYRTON: Who am I? The second of the *Britannia*.

ALL: The second of the *Britannia*?

AYRTON: I was able to escape from the hands of the Australian tribes.

ROBERT: My brother and father are prisoners?

AYRTON: Yes, Robert Grant.

GLENARVAN: And you left them?

AYRTON: Less than three months ago.

MARY: Living, living, right?

AYRTON: Yes, Mary Grant, living.

ALL: Ah! Ah!

ROBERT: Ah! Mr. Ayrton, it's you who will restore to us our father and our beloved brother James!

(Ayrton remains cold under Robert's caresses.)

BOB: Brave lad! I'd like to be his father.

ARABELLA: (astonished) His father?

BOB: (catching himself) No—his—his aunt, milady, his aunt.

AYRTON: Robert Grant, let me find our captain again and I will be content.

GLENARVAN: Look, speak, Ayrton! Tell us truly all that you know.

AYRTON: Milord, after making a lucky crossing around Cape Horn, the *Britannia* experienced a rough storm which half disabled it. It was necessary to flee across the Pacific to the Australian coast. There a new blast of wind, a cyclone, caused it the most serious damage, and it was cast on the rocks, where it was totally lost.

PAGANEL: On what part of the Australian coast?

AYRTON: On the southern part, 200 miles from Melbourne. Several of our unlucky companions perished in the shipwreck, but the Captain, his son, and I reached land. There, some Australians, belonging to nomadic tribes, made us prisoners and they dragged us to the mouth of the Murray River.

DICK: (low to Forster): Bravo! That's where our gang is!

AYRTON: For six months we suffered cruelly, but, by a lucky chance from which our captain and his son were not able to profit, I was able to escape and reach a passenger ship which brought me here, where I am waiting to be repatriated.

GLENARVAN: (shaking Ayrton's hand) I will take care of you! Come aboard the *Duncan*, help us in our search, since you know the country.

ROBERT: Yes, yes, Mr. Ayrton.

AYRTON: I was going to request it of you, Milord. Like you, I no longer want to rest until we've found our captain.

GLENARVAN: (to Ayrton) Finally, Ayrton, what do you advise us to do?

AYRTON: Milord, is the *Duncan* in shape to cross the Pacific?

GLENARVAN: Yes, and by tomorrow it can leave Valparaiso.

AYRTON: Fine! We'll head towards Australia and we'll debark at Melbourne. The *Duncan* will wait in that port until it receives the order to come meet us, while we will go in search of the Australian tribe that must be encamped on the shores of the Murray River.

GLENARVAN: Fine! It's all settled! Tomorrow we will set out.

AYRTON: (to Forster, aside) And in a month, I Ben-Joyce, will command the *Duncan*.

GLENARVAN: Now, Thalcave, it remains for me to thank you and reward you for yours services.

THALCAVE: I repeat to you, I don't want any—

GLENARVAN: But still!

THALCAVE: Allow me to accompany you until the moment in which you find those you are seeking.

GLENARVAN: But how will I be able to thank you for this new service?

THALCAVE: Your friendship.

AYRTON: (aside) What's this savage meddling in for? (to Thalcave) Thalcave, I am the friend of all here!

THALCAVE: Of all? No!

AYRTON: What do you mean?

THALCAVE: (looking him in the face) You are not mine.

MULRAY: (entering and announcing) A messenger from the Governor of Valparaiso requests to speak to you, milord.

GLENARVAN: Show him in. What can he want with us?

AYRTON: (to his comrades) I've succeeded. Tomorrow, during the tumult of the celebration, present yourselves aboard and the *Duncan* is ours!

GLENARVAN: Till later, Ayrton, till later!

(Exit Ayrton, Dick, and Forster.)

MULRAY: (to officer) Here's his Lordship.

OFFICER: Milord, I've been sent to you by his honor the Admiral-Governor of Valparaiso, who begs you to be present at a banquet and ball which will take place at the conclusion of the Festival that is being celebrated tonight by the Chilean miners.

GLENARVAN: We accept this gracious invitation with great pleasure, and I beg you to transmit our thanks to the Governor. My friends, go make yours preparations. (the officer bows) Mulray, please see to it that the *Duncan* is decked out with flags like the other ships in the roadstead.

MULRAY: Your Lordship's orders will be executed.

(Mulray leaves, followed by the officer; Glenarvan leaves. Then Elmira, disguised as a cabin boy, quickly approaches Paganel after making sure Glenarvan and the officer have left.)

PAGANEL: (to himself) On the south coast?

ELMIRA: Sir, sir!

PAGANEL: Huh! What do you want with me, young man?

ELMIRA: I know you. You are Mr. Paganel, the friend of Lord Glenarvan.

PAGANEL: Yes—and so what?

ELMIRA: You seem like a very brave man, sir, and I want you to obtain from milord—that he take me on board.

PAGANEL: As a cabin boy?

ELMIRA: No, sir, no! As a chamber maid.

PAGANEL: Chamber—ma—? What do you mean, young man—you want to become a chamber maid—

ELMIRA: It's that—I am not a young man, sir!

PAGANEL: Ah, bah! You are a—

ELMIRA: Yes, sir, born in Scotland, and I really want to return to my country.

PAGANEL: How, then, does it come about that you find yourself in Chile? And in these clothes?

ELMIRA: I am going to tell you! I had the misfortune of drowning my husband.

PAGANEL: You had? Sit down, then!

ELMIRA: I drowned my husband, yes, sir.

PAGANEL: Why, wretch, explain to me.

ELMIRA: (sweetly) Here it is! You must know first of all that I am jealous.

PAGANEL: Jealous.

ELMIRA: (even more sweetly) Oh very jealous—enough to knife a person.

PAGANEL: Ah!

ELMIRA: (still sweetly) And that person—was my husband—a big—very good-looking—My Bob. I called him Bobbie! He was charming and I loved him; I adored him. That's what made me drown him!

PAGANEL: Drowned—from love. I don't understand.

ELMIRA: You are going to understand. One day we took a trip in a canoe together. And as, that very morning my good-looking little husband had been flirting with the women who passed by, I reproached him.

PAGANEL: Naturally.

ELMIRA: Bit by bit the quarrel envenomed and became so violent that I seized him a bit roughly by the throat! I pushed him, he pushed me! I pushed him back! He pushed me back—and we both fell into the sea.

PAGANEL: And you were able to swim?

ELMIRA: Oh, luckily the wind rushed up my skirts and supported me on the waves—and the rising tide deposited me on the beach.

PAGANEL: And you survived?

ELMIRA: I was saved, sir.

PAGANEL: Bravo! But Bobbie, that unlucky Bobbie! Gulp, gulp, gulp—

ELMIRA: Gulp, gulp! Yes, sir—

PAGANEL: And then?

ELMIRA: Pursued by remorse and fear of being arrested—I went to our lodgings, and dressed myself in a suit and clothes of my poor husband. It looked very becoming on me. Then the idea came to me of expatriating myself, and I left aboard a ship.

PAGANEL: As a cabin boy?

ELMIRA: Yes, sir—and that's how I find myself in Chile! But remorse is pursuing me, alas! And I want to return to Scotland to get myself judged! I intend to expiate my crime, if I am convicted—or marry somebody else if I'm acquitted.

PAGANEL: The *Duncan* is not ready to return to Scotland, but I can get you a letter from Lord Glenarvan to the Captain of an English ship in this port, and at his request he will agree to repatriate you.

ELMIRA: Ah! sir, how kind.

PAGANEL: Wait here. I am going to send you this letter.

ELMIRA: A thousand thanks, sir.

PAGANEL: (looking at her) She's sweet! Young cabin boy, you are nice!

ELMIRA: You are saying?

PAGANEL: I think that your judges will absolve you! As for poor Bobby— Gulp—gulp—gulp—! (leaves)

ELMIRA: Me too, I think they will absolve me! But for that, I would stay here alone. Oh! I am finally going to leave this frightful male attire! I will no longer be forced to clamber like a squirrel in the masts, to smoke this horrible pipe, to put the sailors on board off the track! (pulling a pipe from her pocket) Oh, this pipe! This abominable pipe! It's been useless to break it a hundred times, one after the other, there's always a shipmate quite ready to give me a new one! How amusing for them it would be to see that this disgusts me and they would force me to smoke! Ah, my Bob, you are well avenged.

BOB: (entering) Ah, there's the little sailor in question.

ELMIRA: Someone's coming! Let's dissimulate some more.

BOB: (in a feminine voice) Young man—here's a letter that— (looking at Elmira) a letter which— Ah! God of heaven!

BOB: (aside) What a funny resemblance to my wife!

ELMIRA: (aside) How this girl resembles my husband! (aloud) You were saying, Miss?

BOB: I was saying, young man! You mean—would you have a sister?

ELMIRA: Young lady—would you have a brother?

BOB: (trembling) A brother—me? No, no brother at all— but I have—I had—a wife.

ELMIRA: (moved) A wife! What do you mean, miss— you had a—?

BOB: A pretty little wife!

ELMIRA: Just like me, a pretty little husband.

BOB: Who you resemble enough to be mistaken for.

ELMIRA: Who you resemble feature for feature.

BOB: She had on her right side, near her ear, a birth-mark—a very small birthmark— (passing to the left)

ELMIRA: One day, in a moment of rage he broke a tooth against my fist.

BOB: (looking at her closely) Ah! Great God! But there it is—the birthmark! It's to be found there!

ELMIRA: (looking him in the mouth) Oh—heaven, why it's not there! The tooth is no longer there!

BOB: (falling to his knees) Shade of my wife—is it you that I see under this masculine attire?

ELMIRA: (on her knees, too) Shade of my husband! Is it you who are appearing to me in this feminine dress?

BOB: You know, dearly beloved, that I had no intention of making you drink as much as that!

ELMIRA: You know, oh my adored, that I didn't want to drown you completely! I loved you.

BOB: I cherished you!

ELMIRA: My Bob— My Bobbie!

BOB: My darling Elmira! (pinching her arms and face) O heaven! Why it resists. No—she's not a ghost.

ELMIRA: (prodding him) He's not a phantom!

BOB: No, no, I am really me!

ELMIRA: And I'm me! And I'm me!

BOB: Alive!

ELMIRA: He's alive!

(They hug each other several times and very fast.)

BOB: (shouting) Ah! How nice this is!

ELMIRA: (shouting) Ah! How nice this is!

BOB: (rising) No more frightful terrors.

ELMIRA: (rising) No more horrible remorse!

BOB: (gravely) Ah! If folks knew what remorse is— They would hesitate sometimes to kill their wife.

ELMIRA: You've been faithful to me, right?

BOB: By Jove! I was passing for a woman. And you?

ELMIRA: I was passing for a man.

BOB: It's over! I am retaking my sex and my sailor's attire! No more feminine ribbons. (tearing off his wig) Give me my hat back! (takes it from her and puts it on his head) And I will be able to smoke my pipe. (taking the pipe which Elmira was carrying in the pocket of her vest) She has one of 'em. Oh joy! Got a light?

ELMIRA: (scratching a match) Yes, indeed, yes, indeed! Wait here!

BOB: She's got a light. Ah! It's so long since I've had the happiness of fuming as the French say.

JULES VERNE AND ADOLPHE D'ENNERY * 109

ELMIRA: Well, fume, my little Bob, fume as much as you like!

BOB: (smoking) Hum! What joy, what delight, my wife, my sex and my pipe. I am getting them back all at once!

BOB: (singing)
On the forecastle
Go smell the breeze
On the forecastle
Go smell the wind

BOB and ELMIRA: (together)
On the forecastle
Go smell the breeze
On the forecastle
Go smell the wind

(They dance a jig together.)

ARABELLA: (appearing at the back) Ah! Heavens! (Bob and Elmira separate) Horror! Horror! Abomination!

BOB: Yikes! It's the nervous wreck.

PAGANEL: What's wrong?

ARABELLA: My chamber maid is doing the tango with a young man.

PAGANEL: Why no, that young man is—

BOB: (yelling out) There's no more chamber maid.

ELMIRA: There's no more young man!

ARABELLA: And she's smoking. She's smoking a pipe.

BOB: Well, yes, I am smoking! Yes, I'm laughing, I'm singing and I'm dancing, with this gentleman—who is my wife.

ARABELLA: His wife?

PAGANEL: His wife is "he"?

BOB: There's no more Rebecca, and I am Bob, Bob the sailor, a thousand posts, a thousand starboards, a thousand comrades.

ARABELLA: A man! My chamber maid was a young man! (forcefully) Oh! what a shame, I won't survive it!

PAGANEL: Calm down, milady, calm down.

ARABELLA: No. I don't wish to see such abominations any longer! I want to go back on board, alone, in my cabin! My purse? Where is my purse?

PAGANEL: Here it is, milady.

ARABELLA: Fine. Put in there my fan, my flask, and this little muff—and my parakeet in her cage! Then, my shawl! Hurry up, will you hurry up!

ELMIRA: Hurry up, sir.

(Paganel puts the fan and the flask of smelling salts in the bag, then he places the muff into the cage, and the parakeet into the bag—and finally over it, the shawl, which he squeezes in with punches.)

PAGANEL: It's done, milady, it's done.

ARABELLA: Give me your arm and let's leave.

BOB: Milady.

ARABELLA: Away, wretched woman! And I was thinking of getting her a husband! Let's get going! (to Paganel) Your arm.

PAGANEL: Milady, I've only got two of 'em.

(Paganel holds the cage in one hand and the sack in the other.)

ARABELLA: (taking the cage) Come, my adored parakeet! Come on—ah— (looking at the cage) Come on—what's this?

PAGANEL: (sweetly) The parakeet, Louisa! The pretty parakeet!

ARABELLA: (holding the cage under her eyes) This, this, this!

PAGANEL: That's the muff! What's the muff doing in there?

ARABELLA: (forcefully) Louisa? Where is Louisa? Ah, my God! Could he have possibly? (opens the bag and pulls out the suffocated parakeet) Dead! She's dead!

PAGANEL: Really, what a funny idea to stuff a parakeet in an overnight bag!

ARABELLA: Why, it was you, sir! You are an assassin)

(Arabella falls swooning into a chair.)

PAGANEL: Milady!

ARABELLA: Louisa, my poor Louisa!

PAGANEL: (aside) Could it really be that I am a bit distracted?

CURTAIN

ACT III

Scene 7

THE GOLDEN FESTIVALS OF VALPARAISO

The Stage represents a large, very ornate square in Valparaiso.

Ballet

CURTAIN

ACT IV

Scene 8

AN AUSTRALIAN FOREST

The Stage represents a large forest of trees whose high branches almost hide the entire sky. This forest extends till it is lost in the distance. To the right, large bushes of wood-like ferns. *At Rise*, the Sun hides its light above the wood.

A coach disappears. Ayrton arrives on horseback and dismounts. Following the caravan, Glenarvan, Thalcave, and Robert are in the lead. One wagon enters pulled by Bob who has resumed his masculine clothes, and in which Elmira is lying.

GLENARVAN: We've marched all day and night and will soon arrive. Your advice, Ayrton, is that we ought to camp in this place, isn't it?

AYRTON: Yes, milord. Down there's a prairie where our horses will find something to recover from their labors.

GLENARVAN: Escort the carriage and this wagon into the prairie, and don't wake Lady Arabella and Miss Mary!

BOB: Push, cousin.

MULRAY: (pushing the wagon) Pull, Bob.

GLENARVAN: Poor Lady Arabella, poor Miss Grant! They have endured so many trials during the month since we left Melbourne, and we've been exploring these deserts of lower Australia. (to Ayrton) Decidedly, we will spend the night in this place.

AYRTON: I gave the order to set up camp.

GLENARVAN: (to Robert) You must really be worn out, Robert.

ROBERT: Why no, Milord! Anyway, we're getting closer.

PAGANEL: Certainly we are getting closer! We are finally on a good track. Isn't that true, Mr. Ayrton?

AYRTON: The tribe in which I left Captain Grant cannot be more than twenty miles from here.

GLENARVAN: As for the *Duncan*, we left it at Melbourne to push into these lands, by now it must have arrived, at the mouth of the Murray.

AYRTON: (aside) I'm counting on that indeed!

GLENARVAN: At what distance are we from this place where Wilson should be awaiting us?

AYRTON: Fifty miles at least, milord!

PAGANEL: (astonished) Fifty miles! Come on, that's impossible.

THALCAVE: The air that we are breathing is brought by the sea. Ayrton is mistaken. The coast is much nearer than he said.

PAGANEL: Certainly, and, after my calculations I think I'm able to affirm—

AYRTON: (forcefully) And I maintain, I who crossed through these forests, when I escaped from the hands of the Oneidas—I maintain—that I'm not mistaken.

PAGANEL: Still, my calculations….

AYRTON: Are inexact, sir.

PAGANEL: In that case—it's we who are mistaken, Mr. Thalcave.

GLENARVAN: Ah, it's time we got there! Through an inconceivable fatality, all the animals in our caravan have died, one after the other! There remain to us only two oxen of the ten that comprised the primitive team of the carriage and our horses have fallen on the way!

AYRTON: Accidents of this nature are frequent in the Australian forests. The pasturage is abundant but they produce a venomous herb which kills domesticated animals.

PAGANEL: Yes, yes, the gastrolobium.

AYRTON: That's the one.

PAGANEL: But I thought that the horses and oxen instinctively avoided that herb, and that it occurred only when, by mischance they got mixed in.

AYRTON: Error! To the contrary, they seek it out and eat it avidly.

PAGANEL: (wounded) It seems that today my sense is completely wrong about everything.

THALCAVE: Alone, among us, Ayrton's horse has been preserved.

GLENARVAN: And that is lucky, because, Ayrton, better than any of us can go ahead and reconnoiter the country.

THALCAVE: So be it, but it is not good that since Melbourne the way we have followed was marked by the steps of that horse.

AYRTON: The steps of my horse?

THALCAVE: Yes, the horseshoe bears a clover shape mark which it impresses on the earth and makes it very recognizable. (bending down) Look.

ROBERT: It's true.

AYRTON: (aside) Does this savage notice everything?

PAGANEL: The devil! And they were talking at our departure of numerous escaped convicts, of Ben-Joyce and his gang.

GLENARVAN: Ben-Joyce. Such a track would suffice to guide him if he set himself to follow us?

AYRTON: Milord, it's a frequent custom in this country to shoe horses as I do mine. But, if your Lordship wishes it at the first opportunity I will un-shoe mine.

GLENARVAN: So be it! Let's rejoin Lady Arabella and Miss Grant—and let's be on our guard.

AYRTON: (aside) Nothing! Forster and the others won't come!

PAGANEL: Come on, milord.

(They leave and head towards the wagon. Ayrton remains behind and seems to look in the distance.)

THALCAVE: (who observes him) Is Ayrton remaining here?

AYRTON: Me? No. What's wrong with him to be always looking at me?

(He leaves in his turn followed by Thalcave. Pause. Dick and Forster enter from the right following tracks in the soil. They make a sign and several other convicts enter.)

DICK: (low) That's really the imprint.

FORSTER: Yes, that's clever—it's really Ayrton's horse!

DICK: (looking in the distance) Preparations for encampment? Glenarvan and his men are going to halt in this place. Finally, we've caught up with them. (to a convict) It hasn't been without trouble?

DICK: Since we've been trailing them, twenty times I thought we'd never succeed in finding them.

FORSTER: Silence! Someone.

(All move away.)

DICK: It's him.

ALL: (returning) Ben-Joyce!

AYRTON: (entering) You've been slow in rejoining me.

FORSTER: Leaving Valparaiso at the same time as you— we reached Melbourne a week late! The ship we took didn't run like the *Duncan*! And then, it was necessary to rejoin our companions scattered in the province.

AYRTON: How many are you?

DICK: Here, only ten.

AYRTON: And the rest?

FORSTER: In the forest—at least a thousand.

AYRTON: That's fine. Our plan miscarried at Valparaiso, because instead of coming ashore, the Captain of the *Duncan* remained aboard with his crew.

DICK: But now, by what means can we hope to succeed?

AYRTON: Business is now in a good way. Glenarvan and his companions that I have lured into this forest in search of Oneidas, think they are fifty miles from the coast, when they are, in reality, at such a short distance that if I hadn't stopped their trek in this place, they would soon have been able to reach the littoral and see the masts of their ship. (at this moment, the fern bushes on the left open and let Thalcave's head appear) I can soon be aboard the *Duncan*. At last, I am going to command as master.

FORSTER: What! You?

DICK: You! Ben-Joyce.

THALCAVE: (aside) Ben-Joyce!

AYRTON: A few moments more, I will have a blank check from Glenarvan, and the Captain of the *Duncan* will be placed under my orders. You, Forster, go rejoin our comrades. Twenty of them will follow me and I will receive them aboard the *Duncan*. Go, and do not lose a minute.

FORSTER: Count on me! (leaves)

THALCAVE: (aside) First that one—and the others afterwards.

(Thalcave disappears and slides on the trail of Forster.)

DICK: And us, Ayrton, what must we do?

AYRTON: You stay at a distance in the direction of the coast ready to attack Glenarvan and to exterminate them without pity, once you've seen me again, invested with powers which are going to be given to me. If their resistance is prolonged, we'll soon return and I will come to your aid with the rest of our gang.

(Uproar off. Voices can be heard in the direction the wagon.)

DICK: Listen.

AYRTON: That's the last blow prepared by me which just struck them! Discouragement and terror are spreading amongst them! Leave quickly! Now they are ours! (Dick and the convicts move away) The moment approaches when I am going to become the supreme master aboard the *Duncan*—my ship!

BOB: (calling) Mr. Ayrton! Mr. Ayrton!

AYRTON: Who wants me?

GLENARVAN: A new misfortune.

AYRTON: A misfortune....

GLENARVAN: Our last two oxen have fallen thunderstruck!

AYRTON: They are dead!

PAGANEL: Always the gastrolobium, Mr. Ayrton!

ARABELLA: Impossible now, to continue on our way! What's going to become of us, great God?

ROBERT: Well, we are going on foot until we find the tribe where my father and my brother are prisoners.

PAGANEL: Who will carry our effects and luggage?

BOB: And food stuffs?

GLENARVAN: Ayrton, isn't there in proximity some settlement, some farm, from which we could replace the animals we've lost?

AYRTON: Here, and in the area which surrounds us in the distance, milord—it's desert.

ALL: Desert!

PAGANEL: Alas, yes—desert—unless I am very grossly deceived, I who thought we were only a few miles from the littoral.

MARY: What to do in that case?

AYRTON: (aside) Here we go (aloud) Milord, did my horse succumb as well?

GLENARVAN: No—your horse alone resisted.

PAGANEL: Along amongst all!

AYRTON: Well, milord, there's not an hour, not a minute to lose.

ALL: Get to the point!

AYRTON: It's necessary that one of us, bearing your full powers, knowing the paths and the littoral, go meet your boat! It's necessary that your sailors and your servants come to find us here, bringing new horses, which will allow the caravan to continue on its way.

GLENARVAN: Yes, yes, you're right, Ayrton.

MARY: And this man who will go?

PAGANEL: Invested with full powers! Why only Ayrton knows the route! Only he can mount the lone horse that remains to us!

GLENARVAN: Indeed, but—

PAGANEL: No hesitation, milord! Ayrton alone can save us all.

AYRTON: (aside) Fine! He couldn't speak better if he was one of us!

GLENARVAN: You heard, Ayrton.

AYRTON: I accept the mission, milord, and I am ready to leave.

GLENARVAN: I am going to give you a letter to Wilson which will place the crew of the *Duncan* under your orders.

AYRTON: Fine, milord.

PAGANEL: (to Glenarvan) I am going to write this letter under your dictation! I still have on my person all that's need for that.

GLENARVAN: Do it.

(Paganel takes writing materials from his pocket and prepares to write.)

ARABELLA: Don't make a mistake, at least, eternally distracted one.

PAGANEL: Don't worry this time.

GLENARVAN: Write, Mr. Paganel, write! "Order to Wilson to place the crew of the *Duncan* at the disposition of Ayrton and to execute his instructions in all respects"

PAGANEL: It's done.

GLENARVAN: Give me, so I can sign it.

PAGANEL: Wait so I can reread it since I'm so distracted—as milady says! (reading) "Order to Wilson to put the crew of the *Duncan* at the disposition of Ayrton and to execute his order in all respects"

(Glenarvan signs it.)

PAGANEL: Is it right, Ayrton?

AYRTON: It's right.

GLENARVAN: Bring in the horse.

PAGANEL: And now the address—

(Paganel puts the letter in an envelope which he carefully closes. Ayrton mounts his horse.)

PAGANEL: (giving him the letter) There!

MARY: May God lead you, Ayrton!

ALL: Goodbye! Goodbye!

(Ayrton starts to leave.)

THALCAVE: Stop! Prevent that man from leaving.

GLENARVAN: Ayrton?

THALCAVE: He's not Ayrton; he's called Ben-Joyce!

ALL: Ben-Joyce!

GLENARVAN: Ben-Joyce!

(He rushes at the head of the horse and seizes his bridle. Ayrton discharges his pistol on him and disappears.)

MARY: (rushing to Glenarvan) Ah! Milord!

GLENARVAN: (staggering) Nothing! It's nothing (falling into Thalcave's arms, who makes him sit down) Ben-Joyce!

(At this moment Ayrton reappears and crosses the stage at the back of the forest.)

THALCAVE: My carbine!

(Paganel takes Thalcave's carbine and fires.)

PAGANEL: Missed!

THALCAVE: Oh! I would have killed him!

PAGANEL: Rage made my hand tremble.

GLENARVAN: Ben-Joyce, you said?

THALCAVE: Himself? I was able to kill one of the convicts of his band, but I came back too late to warn you.

GLENARVAN: The *Duncan* lost, its crew soon massacred by these wretches and ourselves, soon at the mercy of convicts! Alas, what to do now, what to do?

MARY: I am going to tell you, milord.

GLENARVAN: You, Miss Mary?

MARY: But above all—we are asking your pardon, my brothers and I, for all the sufferings you endured, you and yours, to attempt to save our dear castaways. We ask your pardon for this wound received for us, alas! for the dangers you have run and those which still menace you! The brave sailors of your crew are going to succumb for us, and those who find themselves here, are, because of us, threatened by death! Pardon us, milord, pardon us!

ROBERT: (kneeling) Pardon us.

GLENARVAN: Stand up! In the name of heaven, stand up.

MARY: No—! Let me finish! Here, death surrounds you on all sides. We must distance ourselves from you most quickly! You must turn back on yours steps, charter a new ship and go back to Scotland. You have done enough for the poor castaways, who are, alas, forever lost, of whom no trace has been found neither in Patagonia nor in Valparaiso, nor in Australia where you are threatened by treachery. Forget then, milord, those who are dear to us, but who are, after all, strangers to you! Forget them, and be blessed in their name for everything you have done!

ROBERT: (weeping) Yes, yes, be blessed.

GLENARVAN: Your thanks and your blessings are accepted, and here I am well paid for past sufferings! But you are advising me to abandon those who, you say, are but strangers to me? Well, may they no longer be so, henceforth! Miss Mary Grant in the face of perils which surround us and of death which threatens us, in the presence of God who hears me, Miss Mary Grant, I have the honor of asking for your hand!

ARABELLA: Fine, my nephew, fine, Edward!

MARY: Milord, I don't know—I must think.

ROBERT: Milord, I am only a child, a poor orphan, perhaps; but whether he be still on earth or in heaven already, I represent my father here, and he thanks you, through my voice, for the great honor that you are doing us, and as for me,—I who will henceforth be your brother—oh! I love you—I love you with all my soul! (shouts from without) The convicts! The convicts!

BOB: (entering) The convicts are approaching! They are going to attack us!

GLENARVAN: Our weapons! Let's defend ourselves, my friends!

ALL: Yes, yes—

GLENARVAN: Let salvation or death come, I am prepared now.

ARABELLA: Fight! They're going to fight! Ah! Great God! Ah! I'm going to faint!

PAGANEL: This is not the moment, milady!

ARABELLA: Well—no! I'm not going to faint. No more nerves, no more weakness. Give me a rifle.

PAGANEL: A rifle!

ARABELLA: Yeas, yes, yes, a rifle! (taking Paganel's) Give me this one, Geographer. (standing ready to fire) Let them come, these bandits! I, too, I'm ready to receive them.

PAGANEL: She's a true rifleman.

(All dispositions ordered by Glenarvan are taken and each awaits the moment to fire. The convicts, numbering around twenty, are captained by Dick. The first shots are exchanged. Thalcave, motionless, fires with the greatest calm. Paganel, his rifle in hand, shoots like a musketeer. Robert strides toward the convicts, fires his revolver, but is going to be bashed by Dick with the butt of his rifle, when he falls by a shot from Arabella. Glenarvan struggles hand to hand, but the convicts being more numerous gain ground and their circle narrows.)

DICK: Courage, comrades, we've got 'em!

ARABELLA: (shooting) Got us? Not yet, scumbag!

(Stubborn defense by Glenarvan and his forces.)

DICK: Be bold! Courage! Forward.

(Shots and shouts of Hurrah are heard from the left. The Duncan's sailors, commanded by Wilson, fire on the convicts.)

WILSON: Forward Clan Malcolm.

(The sailors throw themselves on the convicts who are for the most part killed or take to their heels.)

ALL: Hurrah! Hurrah! Hurrah!

GLENARVAN: Wilson, you, it's you! How'd it happen?

WILSON: Why, milord, I strictly followed your Lordship's orders.

GLENARVAN: My orders?

PAGANEL: Certainly! Written by me!

WILSON: And contained in this letter signed by you.

GLENARVAN: What do you mean?

WILSON: Here they are, milord. (reading) "Seize the bearer of this letter, put him in irons, and rush in all haste to the edge of the forest which runs along the mouth of the Murray."

GLENARVAN: It was in there?

PAGANEL: I knew that honest Ayrton was deceiving us, milord, that we were only a few miles from the coast, and I wrote just the contrary of what you dictated to me. What do you think of that distraction, milady?

GLENARVAN: Yes, my friend, you saved us.

ARABELLA: Ah, Mr. Paganel, now you've expiated many sins. Your hand.

PAGANEL: Both of them, milady, both of them. And I would join my heart to them if you were twenty five years younger! No, if I were twenty-five years older— no, if I—

GLENARVAN: And now, to the *Duncan*! There are no more strangers, Miss Mary. It's my father and my brother I wish to find.

ALL: To the *Duncan*! To the *Duncan*!

CURTAIN

ACT IV

Scene 9

THE MOUTH OF THE MURRAY

GLENARVAN: (extending his arm) Look, look, Mary! There's our dear *Duncan* that we thought was lost to us forever!

MARY: Yes, God be praised!

GLENARVAN: (to Wilson) And that wretch! What did you do with him?

WILSON: He's here. They're bringing him!

GLENARVAN: (to Ayrton) Approach, answer, and don't tremble.

AYRTON: Why should I tremble? Who would dare raise a hand against me or attempt my life? I know where Captain Grant is!

ALL: Ah!

GLENARVAN: Well, speak, and we, who are the arbiters of your fate, we have the right to make you expiate your crimes, perhaps we will be able to grant you mercy and restore you to freedom.

AYRTON: Thanks a lot, milord! But to discuss an agreement or a deal, it's useful to know who is in the other's power. You or I.

GLENARVAN: What are you getting at?

AYRTON: I'm saying that several of those who were fighting against you escaped your blows! I say that they will soon return, accompanied by a hundred others, and that you will be constrained to wait for them, since your ship cannot carry you far from this coast.

GLENARVAN: What will prevent it?

AYRTON: What? Question the captain! He will reply to you that the order he received from you to leave without losing a minute didn't allow him to take on provisions and that you have no more coal in the coal bunkers! The winds are contrary to leaving the bay, and I say to you again, that I am no longer your prisoner! It's you, all of you, who are really mine!

GLENARVAN: Enchain him! Could it be true?

WILSON: (sadly) It is true, milord.

PAGANEL: (looking) Hold on! Perhaps we're not as much the prisoners of this man as he thinks.

GLENARVAN: Explain yourself! Speak!

ALL: Speak!

PAGANEL: (pointing I notice, a small boat down there.

ALL: A small boat!

PAGANEL: A small boat, which no question, belongs to some ship which ought to be in sight.

WILSON: Why, no, you are mistaken.

PAGANEL: What?

WILSON: It's a whale passing out to sea.

GLENARVAN: A whale!

PAGANEL: Well, in default of coal, there's oil, that's a combustible.

GLENARVAN: (forcefully) Yes, you are right! The oil and flesh of that whale will suffice to feed our boilers and make us leave the bay.

BOB: And we will no longer be your prisoners, Mr. Ayrton.

GLENARVAN: Well—do you consent to speak *now*?

AYRTON: No! Let myself bend before you! Never! Never!

SAILORS: (threatening him) To death! To death!

AYRTON: Strike if you dare! I know where Captain Grant is.

GLENARVAN: Take him away. English justice will decide his fate. Go—and now, my friends, to the ship.

ALL: To the ship.

PAGANEL: Well, I won't be sorry to see whale fishing.

CURTAIN

ACT IV

Scene 10

WHALE FISHING

The stage is occupied entirely by the sea. A whale can be seen in the distance, gradually; it approaches, enlarges, beats the water with its formidable tail, blows in the air, and opens its enormous mouth garnished with fangs.

Paganel, Robert, and Mulray, come in a whaler. Paganel, in the front, brandishes his harpoon. Mulray, in the rear, steers with the rudder.

PAGANEL: Hold on! She's just disappeared around the point of the island! Ah! There she is! A magnificent whale!

ALL: She's coming back!

PAGANEL: Forward, Mulray, close in, close in! Attention!

WILSON: She doesn't see us!

PAGANEL: Luckily! What, old sea wolf, are you ignoring us at the most propitious moment?

(The whale approaches and Paganel hurls his harpoon which lodges in the whale's flank.)

PAGANEL: Get back, everybody.

ALL: Get back!

(The whale recoils—then, after having struck the water with its tail, cause Paganel to fall into the sea, and dives as the same time.)

MULRAY: How unfortunate!

ROBERT: (ready to jump) Ah, I can save him!

MULRAY: Hold on! Hold on!

(The whale resurfaces little by little. Paganel, swimming, clings to the beast.)

MULRAY: Ah! God be praised! You gave us a fright.

PAGANEL: It's nothing. A little distraction which was worth a superb blow to me, hold on. A single hit with the harpoon sufficed! Why no! It has a second in it's flank! (tears out the second harpoon) Wait—what do I read? "Captain Grant 1877"

ROBERT: That's quite recent.

PAGANEL: "Captain Grant, Balker Island" Bal—Balk—Balker!

ALL: Balker Island.

PAGANEL: An island situated two hundred miles from here!

ROBERT: My father! My father!

ROBERT and MULRAY: Found! Found!

PAGANEL: A singular man, your father; who puts his letters in the belly of a shark; and who sends his visiting card on the flank of a whale.

GLENARVAN: Robert, within three days we will be at Balker Island.

ALL: Hurrah! Hurrah! Hurrah!

CURTAIN

ACT V

Scene 11

BALKER ISLAND

The stage represents a beach on the island. To the left, high cliffs already blanched with snow. To the right ice floes entangled with each other. At the foot of the cliff a miserable hut made of some strips of canvas which support a bit of worn sail cloth. Around the beach, the sea, already encumbered by ice floes. Half day. The horizon is slightly inflamed by the last rays of sun which is about to disappear.

James is stretched out in the hut. Grant, near him, is occupied by engraving a few characters on the butt of his rifle. Both are dressed in rags. A little wood fire is near the hut.

GRANT: Come on, courage! Courage!

JAMES: Yes, father.

GRANT: Eighteen months abandoned! Eighteen months of unheard of sufferings! (looking at James stretched out) Ah, that wretched Ayrton knew quite well what he was doing by leaving me my son. It multiplies my tortures! My child! My poor child!

JAMES: Father! I'm really thirsty.

GRANT: Alas! Fever is devouring him. A little melted snow is all I have to appease him. (amasses a little snow, which he places in an iron cup, and melts it over the fire) Drink, James, drink!

JAMES: Thanks, father. (falling back on his couch)

GRANT: Each day his strength diminishes. I see it plainly! But he pities me, he hides his tears from me, he doesn't tell me all that he suffers. Oh, my heart is bursting. (tears choke him, he half falls on a rock, then rises) No more wood! This is our last fire. The winter we have endured in this horrible desert has devoured all that this arid isle could produce. And here's the second winter beginning, bringing with it this frightful polar night. This four-month night. Already the ice floes are piling up in every direction, the ice pack envelops us and is going to imprison us anew, tearing our last hope from us of seeing some ship. What's going to become of us this time? Ah! God has no pity on us!

JAMES: (who's got up, dragging himself towards his father) Father, don't cry! Don't despair! I feel better. A little nourishment will set me up. There are still some birds on the island.

GRANT: I am going to try to bring some back.

JAMES: Yes, father, and promise me not to cry any more! I tell you I have good hope!

GRANT: My James!

JAMES: I am certain they will come to our assistance! You know quite well the bottle you cast in the sea! The document it enclosed must have fallen into the hands of generous, brave men! They are perhaps now seeking us. Don't despair, father! (staggering) Don't despair.

GRANT: (with terror) You are ill—you are staggering.

JAMES: (even more feebly) No—no—I'm not ill—I—I— a bit weak, that's all.

(James falls into his father's arms.)

GRANT: James! My child! My dear child!

JAMES: I'm going—back to my bed—while you go— hunt for the two of us! But not too far—okay?

GRANT: Oh! no, I won't go too far! I still tremble over that miserable Burke. Several times he came right here to steal what provisions we have. Even this small amount of precious brandy which I've kept— and a few drops would be able to revive you, my poor James.

JAMES: Don't worry! It's been a long while since he re-appeared! Perhaps he left the island on some floating debris—or perhaps he's dead, alas!

GRANT: James, you are shivering.

JAMES: Carry me to our cabin! I—I....

GRANT: James! My James—oh heaven! He's losing consciousness. My God, is he going to die? Are you doing to tear him from me? Ah! It's this cold, this horrible cold which is killing him. (takes James into the hut, places him on the bed and takes off his own jacket to cover his son) He seems more calm. Yes, he's sleeping. Perhaps a few hours of sleep will make this fever that's preying on him fall! Oh! My poor child, I wanted to associate you in the glory of my discoveries and I have only associated you in my misery and my sorrows. Pardon me, pardon me! Come on, let's go before the last birds abandon these parts.

JAMES: (in his sleep) Mary! Robert! Yes, yes—it's you!

GRANT: (coming close) He's dreaming of his brother, of his sister! What are my children doing? Ah! Unfortunate father! Whose heart at the same time feels the sufferings of the one who is here and all the despair of those who are weeping elsewhere. (casting a last glance on the sleeping James) Let's go.

(Grant leaves, crossing through the rocks. James, in prey to the delirium of the fever, is turning in his bed and rises.)

JAMES: Father! Father! Come with me! Ah! We've been rescued at last! We are saved! (getting out of his bed) We've left this deserted and frozen island! See those trees, those flowers, this fine sunlight which warms us up! It's spring! It's spring! (a little snow begins to fall and the light on the horizon diminishes) Ah! There— there's Mary and Robert! I am seeing you again! I am hugging the two of you! How good it is to find our- selves together! Father! They've come and we are going to leave with them! Hurry, father, hurry up! The ship is there! It's going to take us back to our dear country. (rising and looking around) Father, where are you? Where are you then? The ship is waiting for us! Ah! Heaven—it's going to go away—it's raising anchor! Stop! Stop! Stop! It's leaving—it's leaving without us! It's disappearing down there—down there! And the ice floe that's closing and death—death is coming. (falls exhausted)

(Burke enters by the left. He is dressed in skins. A gourd hangs at his side. A hatchet is in his hand. His beard is un- cut. He has the appearance of a wild beast. He runs across the stage without seeing the child.)

BURKE: It's him—down there! There he is, this Grant. (waving his axe) Ah! If he were not better armed than I am! Patience! powder and bullets will be exhausted. Ah! You had me whipped till I bled! Oh! I will avenge myself! Perhaps they still have some provisions. I have to have them! (noticing the fire) Fire! They've got fire while I'm croaking with cold! (with a violent blow of his foot he disperses the fire) Come warm yourself now! (messing with the hut) Nothing! No provisions! Where are they hiding, then? Ah! Ah! A hut for them! I don't want it! (tears the strips of sail which support the poles, then the poles break) Do I have a shelter to protect me? They shan't have more than I do. Yes, yes, pillage, pillage, kill, if you meet them! (runs across the stage and stumbles over the child with his foot) The son, the child of my enemy! Ah! How I am going to avenge myself! Yes, the son, while waiting for the father! (approaching James, hatchet raised) Heavens! He's sleeping. Ah, why no! Wake him up first! I want him to know that it's I who am killing him, I who will be avenged on him for what Harry Grant did to me. (leaning over James) I want to see the contortions of his face, and hear his last cry of sorrow. I want to feel his quivering flesh, under the pressure of my fingers as mine quivered under the blows of the whip that his father inflicted on me. Wake up, you, come on!

JAMES: (coming to, but still in delirium) Ah, it's you! You've come back, father.

BURKE: Me! Your father! Ah! You are going to see. Come on, open your eyes. (raises him up by a hand and places the other at the child's throat) Look—look me carefully in the face and die!

JAMES: Your hand! Yes, give me your hand, father. (takes Burke's hand) Let me place it on my heart so you can feel its last beat! Father, I am going to die!

BURKE: Die? He's going to die! Well, all the better, fate is doing the job for me! I won't have the bother of killing him—and with him I will see extinguished the last joy, the last hope of Harry Grant.

JAMES: We will find each other together again in heaven!

BURKE: Heaven! Bah! The dumb things they say to kids! (laughing) Ah! Ah! Heaven! (looking at James) How pale he is. (coming close to him) He's young, he hasn't got the strength to suffer, no, he doesn't have the strength! Heavens!—see the tears running from his eyes! Is he truly going to die?

JAMES: Die, yes! But first, we have to forgive, father—forgive everybody.

(James takes Burke's hand and presses it against his lips.)

BURKE: (wanting to withdraw his hand) His lips are burning my hand! Yes! Yes! He seems to be suffering greatly. (with rage) Well—what are his sufferings to me? Can this move me, me, Burke? Come off it! One would say he's choking. (then, softly) After all, he wasn't the one who had me beaten.

JAMES: Tell me that you forgive all the sailors on the *Britannia*. Ayrton—and Burke, also, father.

BURKE: He's thinking of me at the moment of dying—of me, the enemy of his father—and himself. Ah, sonofabitch! These honest folk! They have secrets to affect your heart.

JAMES: If the two of us die, Burke will remain alone—on this little island—all alone—facing God!

BURKE: (moved) God! He's talking the way my mother talked to me—when I was very little and sick like him! But—what's going on in me? (taking the child in his arms and supporting him) I've seen men murdered a hundred times! But not like this— Oh, no—not like this!

JAMES: Support me! No, on my knees! Put me on my knees so I can make my last prayer.

BURKE: On his knees—his—his last prayer— Come on—am I going to start weeping now? (as he puts the child on his knees, he himself kneels) Well, yes—here I am weeping now! I'm weeping.

JAMES: Repeat with me: My God, forgive me for our trespasses—

BURKE: (weeping) Oh! No!

JAMES: Why, repeat, will you! I cannot hear— My God—!

BURKE: (hesitating) My—my God!

JAMES: Forgive us our trespasses!

BURKE: Forgive us our trespasses!

JAMES: As we pardon those who trespassed against us.

BURKE: As we pardon those who trespassed against us!

(James collapses exhausted.)

BURKE: His hand is frozen. Fainted. (bursting out) Ah! Hell's Bells, I don't want him to die— I don't want it! Have to save him—have to save him! What to do! It's the cold, exhaustion, that he's dying from! Some Brandy. I have theirs that I stole from them! I can give him back a little. (takes his gourd, half opens James' lips and makes him drink a few drops) There now, his cheeks are less pale.

JAMES: (coming to) Ah! That helps me! Strength is coming back to me a little!

BURKE: (with gentleness) Come on, some courage, kid, courage!

JAMES: Yes—I—I feel I'm better! Thanks, father—thanks— (recognizing Burke) Burke!

BURKE: Child!—child! Don't suspect anything of me—! I am no longer your enemy! No, no—my heart has no more hate—for you, at least!

JAMES: Nor for my father, right?

BURKE: Nor for (forcefully) Well, yes, neither for you, nor for him! Are you satisfied?

JAMES: (embracing him) Ah! Burke—my friend.

BURKE: (weeping) Poor child, poor child. Come on—decidedly—I think it's good—to be good!

(Grant reappears at the right, rifle in hand and at first doesn't see James and Burke.)

GRANT: Nothing! Nothing more in this island. (noticing Burke) Burke—you here—wretch! (aims at him)

JAMES: (dragging himself before his father) Father! Father! He helped me! He brought me back to life.

GRANT: Him—

BURKE: You can kill me, Harry Grant. I won't defend myself!

GRANT: Could heaven have touched your soul? Has it made this miracle? At the moment when it seemed to abandon us completely.

BURKE: I am repenting. Do with me what you wish.

GRANT: You renounce your past and you have succored my child! Burke, perhaps—I was too severe and too harsh, in punishing you aboard my ship.

BURKE: I was culpable—but no, Captain—

GRANT: Now, there's no more captain here nor sailor. There's only two men equal before God. (Burke, confused, walks away weeping) Burke, you will be our companion, our friend.

BURKE: No, captain! Your slave. (kneels)

GRANT: Get up! We will struggle together against misery—against death.

BURKE: Master, we will struggle against this terrible cold, and this four-month-long night.

GRANT: Alas! Heaven made a moment of hope shine in my eyes! Some days ago a whale was stranded on the beach. I attacked it. I struck it with my harpoon.

BURKE: Yes, yes, I saw it! I touched that harpoon on which you'd engraved your name and that of our island—Captain Grant, Balker Island, while to finish it you were without doubt—gone to seek another weapon.

GRANT: And when I returned, the tide, pushed by a furious wind—was in ahead of time.

BURKE: And the whale, set back afloat, was able to escape.

(At this moment the firing of a cannon is heard in the distance. Burke rises and supports James who has not the strength to walk. Grant rushes up the rocks of the cliff.)

GRANT: A cannon shot!

(On the horizon, carving its way through the last light from the sky, a ship is seen passing slowly.)

BURKE: Captain! A ship! A ship!

GRANT: God has heard us! We are saved, my friends.

BURKE and JAMES: We are saved!

GRANT: I will see my children! My country!

JAMES: What joy, what happiness!

GRANT: But the boat cannot see us! It's firing on the ice floe to break a path through the ice. Is it really trying to get close to us?

(Two more cannon shots.)

BURKE: A signal. We must make a signal!

GRANT: How?

JAMES: Father—your rifle!

GRANT: Yes! Yes—

(Grant goes back up on the rock and discharges his rifle twice into the air. But the ship moves away little by little, and the horizon narrows from the displacement of the ice.)

GRANT: It didn't hear us. (shouting) Help!

BURKE and JAMES: Help! Help!

GRANT: Nothing more.

(The snow falls very abundantly.)

JAMES: Alas! To have glimpsed rescue, safety and happiness! And to fall back into despair and death.

(Four cannon shots.)

BURKE: The cannon again?

GRANT: And much closer this time.

BURKE: Look! Look! Captain! The ice is breaking up—!

JAMES: My god! My God! Could you have had pity on us
at last.

BLACKOUT

ACT V

Scene 12

BALKER ISLAND II

The breaking up of the ice continues. Day appears and the horizon reflects the first light of the new sun.

BURKE: And there the sun's returning

GRANT: The sea is free.

JAMES: Ah! Look, look, papa!

(The ship has appeared between the ice floes. A small boat is approaching the island.)

ACT V

Scene 13

THE MIDNIGHT SUN

ROBERT: (shouting) Father! James! Father!

GRANT: It's them—my children.

JAMES: My sister—my beloved brother!

GRANT: Robert! Dear Mary! But how were you able to reach this island?

ARABELLA: Your document, captain!

PAGANEL: Yes, your document! But it must be admitted you have a singular manner of correspondence! To take sharks and whales for postmen.

MARY: Father—Lord Glenarvan, your savior.

GRANT: Be thanked and blessed, milord. You've returned a father to his children.

GLENARVAN: And a great sailor to England.

CURTAIN

ABOUT FRANK J. MORLOCK

FRANK J. MORLOCK has written and translated many plays since retiring from the legal profession in 1992. His translations have also appeared on Project Gutenberg, the Alexandre Dumas Père web page, Literature in the Age of Napoléon, Infinite Artistries.com, and Munsey's (formerly Blackmask). In 2006 he received an award from the North American Jules Verne Society for his translations of Verne's plays. He lives and works in México.

Lightning Source UK Ltd.
Milton Keynes UK
13 April 2011

170842UK00001B/216/P